AF540784

BANNED

BANNED

A Social Media Trial

Boria Majumdar

London · New York · Sydney · Toronto · New Delhi

First published in India by Simon & Schuster India 2024

Copyright © Boria Majumdar, 2024

No reproduction without permission.

The right of Boria Majumdar to be identified as author of this work has been asserted by him in accordance with Section 57 of the Copyright Act 1957.

1 3 5 7 9 10 8 6 4 2

Simon & Schuster India
818, Indraprakash Building,
21, Barakhamba Road,
New Delhi 110001.

www.simonandschuster.co.in

Simon & Schuster: Celebrating 100 Years of Publishing in 2024

Hardback ISBN: 978-81-970426-3-8
eBook ISBN: 978-81-970426-5-2

Typeset in India by SÜRYA, New Delhi
Printed and bound in India by Replika Press Pvt. Ltd.

Simon & Schuster India is committed to sourcing paper that is made from wood grown in sustainable forests and support the Forest Stewardship Council, the leading international forest certification organisation. Our books displaying the FSC logo are printed on FSC certified paper.

No part of this publication may be reproduced, transmitted or stored in a retrieval system, in any form or by any means, electronic, mechanical, photocopying, recording or otherwise, without the prior permission of the publisher.

This book is sold subject to the condition that it shall not, by way of trade or otherwise, be lent, resold, hired out, or otherwise circulated, without the publisher's prior consent, in any form of binding or cover other than that in which it is published.

To my family. No social media trial can break us ever.

And

To all who have felt powerless against the entitled.

This is for them.

Contents

1

YPU Controversy

YPU. A term that starts with one of the lesser-used letters in the English language, and three letters that are seldom used in this configuration. But strung together, they had the power to nearly destroy a life, and deeply damage a career built with two decades of hard work. Why do I write this now? Do I not know that I will be abused and trolled relentlessly once this book is published? Have my family and I not had enough? More than half a million abusive tweets in the week between February 20, 2022 and February 26, 2022. Weren't those enough? Why do I want to put my loved ones, and myself, through that again?

Also, why now? Why did I not speak up earlier? When scores of journalists asked me to talk about the ban, I stayed silent. In fact, I didn't utter a word on the issue in the last two years. I waited for the ban to be lifted, endured in silence for 730 days.

Why? If there was a story to be told, why wait?

I have written many books. Words are my friends. But never have I felt as apprehensive before writing something as now. Why would I revisit the nightmare? Why do I want to confront that time in my life again? The wrongs heaped on me. Especially now that things are going well for me, and for Revsportz, a company that is no less to me than a child.

As human beings, we are guided by certain principles. Each of us have our own set of values. To be told that you are a bully, that you have threatened a cricketer and intimidated him merely for an interview, when you have not, compels one to set the record straight. My mother, now 74, became severely anxious and depressed, and my wife was harassed and abused on social media. Even if one person reads it, it's important that I put my story out there. I write this for my family and for myself, knowing that it might well invite another avalanche of vitriol.

Wait. Is this just for Sharmistha, my wife, and Roopa, my mother? What about my 10-year-old daughter, who was eight then, who couldn't quite comprehend yet possibly knew something was very wrong at home? She wasn't old enough to comprehend the gravity of the situation—and thank God for that—but could she not sense that her father, a strong and positive person by nature, was all but broken? Could she sense her mother putting on her bravest face, and her grandmother on the verge of a breakdown? Can you imagine the impact on the mind of an eight-year-old?

Mental health, anyone?

So, yes, I had to write this book. Frankly, I don't give a *%*%

about the trolls. For days and months, I sought validation. I tried to make people understand that what was in the public domain was not the truth. There was another side to it, my side, which should have been heard at that point. Entire articles and opinion pieces were written even in well-respected dailies without asking for a response from me. Public sympathy was not in my favour. The Cricketer who had represented the national team for over a decade, was always more powerful than I on social media. His narrative would naturally find mass acceptance. Needless to say, I never had a chance. National-team players in India are demi-gods. So when he came out against me in public alleging that I had threatened him, my truth was quickly turned around. That he did not take my name in public did not help my case—if anything, it gave the whole episode more fuel and fire when there started a frantic guessing game over who it could be. He did, of course, give my name to the committee, and convinced them that he was feeling 'unsafe', so much so that he had come to the airport (to make the trip to depose before the committee) in a different car from his own, and that he feared for his future.

I last spoke to the man on February 13, 2022, when I congratulated him after an Indian cricket franchise bought him at that year's auction, a week before he posted my WhatsApp messages on social media. Why did he allow a week to pass before he posted those messages on social media? And, how was I (and not anybody else) responsible for his or his family's subsequent mental trauma, as he had claimed before the committee? We had known each other well over a decade. On what basis could anybody say that I had engineered his trauma days after I had sent him my last WhatsApp messages, and why wasn't that statement questioned?

I have not survived in my profession of journalism for over two decades by threatening and bullying people, and still less players and athletes who I consider national treasures. A middle-class Bengali with a set of values I live by, and a young daughter almost the age of The Cricketer's own child. How could I be held responsible for anybody else's feelings of insecurity or any rumours that he might have heard about losing his place within the national cricket set up? In fact, that it will happen was written by another journalist and not me. I did not have any contact with him after February 13 and I certainly did not float those rumours. How could someone get away with such a preposterous suggestion? And how was it believed?

Justice?

What was told to the committee was not in my presence and I did not have a chance to directly counter the allegations or pose any questions to him in the presence of the committee. No cross examination. Let the recordings of the testimonies before the committee, his and mine, be disclosed. The sessions were recorded, and my side, and my defence of myself, should be in the public domain.

Repeatedly, The Cricketer asked (in his tweets and media interviews) why I didn't apologise, or show any remorse for what I had done. Apologise for what? For not accepting the charges thrust on me? Or admitting to the guilt that I was being forced to concede to? In fact, the committee members could tell you that during my own appearance before them I demanded that

The Cricketer should apologise for the trauma that his actions had caused me and my family. I still feel that he should.

The media fed on The Cricketer's narrative and this in turn forced a witch-hunt on me. The Cricketer told the committee that I had pressured, and by implication, intimidated him for the past 2-3 years. While he steered clear of naming me in public on this issue, his media declarations effectively stoked the fire of this controversy by suggesting repeatedly that I was remorseless and unapologetic, and that drove an unabated avalanche of social media abuse and negativity at myself and my family. I was pronounced guilty even before my story was heard. When the troll army had taken over, what chance did a start-up entrepreneur, toiling to set up a media company, have anyway? The ban that followed was almost inevitable.

To set the record straight, once and for all. I did not threaten The Cricketer. And that's why I decided to write this book. I decided to take on the trolls and the hate army, and deal with the toxic online fan culture that has taken over Indian cricket. If you question an Indian cricketer of any stature as part of your media job, your parentage is questioned. Why?

In the past, Indian cricket legends like Sunil Gavaskar, Kapil Dev and Sachin Tendulkar have faced uncomfortable questions from journalists. Kapil's shot against England in the 1987 World Cup semi-final, which may have cost India the game, was debated for weeks, and he even lost the captaincy as a result. But the journalists who did those stories were not called names as a result.

What has changed now? Have we become more intolerant as

a society? What does it say when we don't even wish to listen to the other side? Millions saw only the victim card, without having a clue that the same individual had sent me multiple messages in the past, requesting me to put out his side of the story in the media in different situations. Asking me to not reveal his name as the source of my information, so that he wouldn't be in the Apex Body's bad books. I have quoted from some of those WhatsApp messages in this book, for the record. It is time to tell the full story.

The Cricketer is saying on record that he had felt threatened by my attitude towards him for over 2-3 years. When someone is such an obnoxious bully, why would you send them messages saying 'Don't write you have got this from me' (inside information) or suggest they put out your side of a story? Instead of putting me in my place, why would a cricketer of stature tolerate such behaviour? Why tweet to promote it? Why grant me multiple interviews? And most importantly, why pick that particular date—19 February—for posting my WhatsApp messages on social media.

Does any of that make sense? And would it have made the slightest difference if I pointed these things out in February 2022? How can you stop the tide when over 100,000, often nameless and faceless trolls are abusing you online every day? How was I to get a fair hearing when even my fellow journalists had pronounced me guilty without bothering to check my side of the story, a basic of journalistic ethics?

I worked in an organisation for nine long years, heading sport and putting in my best every single day. Someone who replaced me in that same organisation called one of my RevSportz colleagues at least five times in a day, inviting him to go and speak against me on his show. Not once was I called and asked to put forth my version of events. Two sides to every tale? Not here. Instead, Debasis Sen, my colleague, was harassed by a fellow journalist for inside details on what I was doing after I was accused by The Cricketer. What was my plan? Could he please tell them that I was indeed guilty! This was from the same media house where I had worked for nine years, with whose owners I still share a rapport. I wonder if they even knew what was going on!

But then, there is always the truth. Each of us has a voice and I decided to stand up to the trolls. To wrongdoing. I emerged from the endless dark tunnel of a media trial because I had my family with me. And my team. I owe it to them to put out the real story.

I mustered the courage to respond. And yes, I did not bully anyone. Or threaten them. Not once. I did help The Cricketer, on many occasions. When he was at the National Cricket Academy (NCA) recuperating from an injury, he had sent me multiple WhatsApp messages seeking help, i.e., to put out something favourable about him in the media. When his manager came to my house and said: 'Do something for_____da', I agreed.

Finally, the last time when I spoke to The Cricketer, on the evening of February 13, 2022—within moments of the cricket franchise drafting him—there were other people in the room that heard me say that we should celebrate him. We do not have many players from Bengal in the cricket T20 league, I told him, and this would be a good time to speak and celebrate. Trisha Ghosal, my colleague, even said to me at the time that everyone was tired after covering the league's auction through that entire day and that we should just let it be. She was unwell and it was a fair request. I was the one who insisted that we interview and celebrate The Cricketer because he was one of our own, a fellow Bengali. In fact, the next day, I interviewed the head coach of the very same franchise that had drafted him. And one of my questions to him, still out there in the public domain, was whether the franchise would give more opportunities to The Cricketer, for he was good enough and deserving of the chance.

And then, within days, I was accused of trying to end the career of the very same man. The logical question that nobody asked was, what power or authority did I have to do so? I had asked the coach of his franchise, why he shouldn't get more opportunities. This was just days before The Cricketer put out his first tweet against me. He did so a little after 10 pm on February 19, 2022. I noticed then that the date on those WhatsApp messages was blurred out in the tweets, giving people the impression that they had been sent that very same day, not a week before, in the context of the league's auction. Nobody asked why that was done. Why indeed it was necessary to blur the date on my previous messages before they were posted in the public domain? Within minutes, I was Indian cricket's public enemy no. 1. A bully.

How did all this start and how did it spiral out of control within hours? This is that story.

2

Guilty Till Proven Innocent

How the Issue Unfolded

It was 10:13 pm on February 19, 2022 when Kushan, who heads cricket coverage for a national news agency and is one of my closest friends, sent me a WhatsApp message asking: 'What's happening? What is this?' Below his message was The Cricketer's tweet, along with screengrabs of WhatsApp messages sent by me a week before, which gave the impression that I had sent the texts to him in the context of his getting dropped from the Indian Test team that very same day, a week after the league's auction.

The Cricketer put out his tweet on February 19. The reproduced WhatsApp messages that accompanied the tweet had *no date*, something which is always there in a WhatsApp message. What happened to the date part of the messages? It is a question that I raised before the committee? And a very serious question it was, the moot question if any in this whole matter. Why was it necessary to blur or obscure that part of the message before it was put out on a public platform? In any case, it was a violation of my privacy as an individual to have my private messages with another individual splashed across social media without my consent, as my lawyer tells me. The messages, for the record, were *actually* sent on February 13, *but* they were tweeted out by the Cricketer on February 19. For every layperson, the impression the tweet therefore gave was that the messages *were sent* on February 19, within hours of The Cricketer's omission from the Test squad. It's only logical that irate fans would assume that my WhatsApp messages and The Cricketer's subsequent reaction on social media were linked to that. That I had pressed him for a reaction on his being dropped from the squad.

The reality, however, was profoundly different, and which has so far been obscured in the public domain. Here are some questions for The Cricketer before I go on to address what happened:

Did I send him even a single message related to his omission from the Test team? Did I ask for an interview a week *before* or immediately after he was dropped? Did I say a word about his India career? Did I not send the messages the day he was picked by the cricket franchise, to celebrate his cricket league contract?

When I received Kushan's message, I was in my bedroom after a long day's work, and was dozing off. It took me a few seconds to even comprehend what the message meant, for such a tweet was beyond my wildest imagination. What was being portrayed—that I was trying to 'bully' him? When I realised what the tweet implied, my first thought was to call The Cricketer and ask him what was up. Like I would any person I knew well. But then, sense prevailed and I held back apprehending that having put out such a tweet, he might also declare that I had called and threatened him, after I had seen his tweet. I realised anything was possible.

To be honest, I was confused. Not scared, but confused, because I hadn't yet realised the gravity of the situation. In my mind, I was clear that I hadn't done anything on the lines of what was being implied. Hence, the thought that it could derail my career hadn't even occurred to me. The next morning, I decided to speak to my wife, and showed her the tweet. She was grim after she read it, and for the first time, I realised what this could mean, at a time when social media outrage rules our lives.

Within the hour of the first tweet, I had started trending. And each response was full of abuse. A cricketer of repute had put out a tweet, and it had played on fans' sentiments. It had to be a Gospel truth. Why would someone like The Cricketer, who has played many Test matches for India, lie? Why would anyone even try to comprehend why indeed he put out those messages?

One of my early calls, the next morning, was to a lawyer, who asked me if The Cricketer had named me in the tweets. When I said no, I was asked to lie low and not say a word. 'If need be, we will put out a statement clarifying the whole matter,' she said. Within the next couple of hours, the number of tweets against me had swelled to the thousands, and I got a call from a senior cricket official of Bengal asking me to not go to Eden Gardens to watch India play the West Indies. I was told that I could be suspended.

'Suspended from what?' I remember asking him. He had no real answer. He merely said that it was in my best interests to stay quiet and let the issue fade away. Social media jumps from one issue to another, and I wasn't important enough for people to stay glued to this. That's when I called a top cricket administrator, someone I have known for three decades. He told me that he was concerned about what had been put out by The Cricketer and asked me what had really happened. He was leaving for London the following day, and asked why I couldn't meet The Cricketer, who I knew well too, and explain that he had clearly misunderstood me. This cricket administrator was also aware that The Cricketer's manager had come to my house a week earlier to plan a media series involving my company and The Cricketer and some of the other players that he managed. 'Speak to his manager and close the matter,' was the gist of the advice from him.

But then, the water had already started to rise over my head. Tense, anxious and alarmed, it was a night I will never forget. Instinctively, I kept checking Twitter, and each time I did, the number of tweets abusing me had swelled exponentially. Over time, my family was drawn into it. There were abuses posted below pictures of my wife, and one of the tweets mentioned my daughter, and how unfortunate she was to be born to a father like me. While I hadn't been named by The Cricketer, it was apparent to most that he had referred to me.

In the screengrab tweeted by The Cricketer, I had accidentally spelt the word 'YOU' as 'YPU'. Many had figured out that it was a common typographical error on my part, and hence it had to be me that had sent the messages. Even those who didn't know who The Cricketer was talking about had joined in the tide of abuse regardless. By then, some notable cricketers who I had known well for years had also tweeted on the issue. Each tweet added to the tide of wrath, and by 5 am the following morning, it was evident that I was facing one of the biggest challenges of my life.

I was guilty till I could prove my innocence, not the other way round.

My first calls that morning were to two ex-Bengal cricketers, one of them my cohort and another a senior I have a great regard for, and two of my close friends. Both were stunned to hear that I was the alleged harasser, and said they would try and help resolve the matter. The senior of them, who was commentating on a domestic game, even asked me if I wanted him to speak to The Cricketer, for after all, the cricket fraternity was like a big family, and he would try and help ease the matter. The other, on his part, asked me to write down the exact chronology of events and keep it handy, in case I needed to put out my side of the story. Both asked me to stay quiet and not react publicly.

By mid-morning on February 20, the mainstream media had picked up the story. It was a juicy tale—an experienced cricketer alleging harassment by a senior journalist. Just the kind of story that sells. And because I hadn't been named, the story allowed for speculation as well. It could be kept alive, and for platforms that needed content, it was a gold mine.

While many of the reports speculated on the identity of the person, others conjectured that it was me based on the word 'YPU'. And as each story came out, the hatred grew exponentially.

How dare I threaten a respectable gentleman like The Cricketer? How dare I write that he had to give me an interview, failing which I would supposedly ruin his national career? Or even his prospects in franchise cricket. Some even said that I should be lynched and put in jail because I had tried to hurt The Cricketer's prospects.

Not one of these journalists, however, bothered to call me and check if I had something to say on the matter, which is a basic courtesy in journalism. At noon on February 20, I finally called The Cricketer's manager, who had visited me at home a few days earlier to plan a media series involving The Cricketer and some other cricketers. He was well aware of my previous support for this Bengal cricketer, and especially my support of him as a fellow Bengali. There was a WhatsApp group with the said manager and my partners, where a number of messages had detailed our promotional plans involving the cricketers he managed. Those messages are still with me.

The least I expected from the same person was to say that there had been a misunderstanding. To my utter astonishment, he said, 'The way I see_____da, he won't lie.' In a call which lasted well over 20 minutes, he kept saying that this was something between The Cricketer and I, and it was best if he was kept out of it. It was a sign of how things would play out over the coming weeks.

When I told the manager that he knew full well I hadn't been in touch with The Cricketer since the day of the cricket league's auction, and that the WhatsApp screenshots tweeted out by The Cricketer conveyed a radically different picture, his answer was,

'That, I don't know.' Clearly, he had chosen to distance himself from the issue, and wasn't willing to help. This, after he had called me multiple times in the past seeking my support to promote his athletes, and met me on several occasions to discuss how he could collaborate with RevSportz to plan events for the cricketers he managed. I have a recording of this call with him.

By then, I was desperate. I needed someone to stand by me and say that I was actually telling the truth. I had known the then President of Bengal's Apex Body for 20 years, and he is someone I considered family. He was the man in-charge of the India-West Indies game, and it was very likely that he would meet The Cricketer at the Eden Gardens. I had learnt the ropes of Indian cricket under his father, and felt he was someone I could surely turn to. He did take my call, and having heard my side of the story for over 20 minutes, he promised to speak to The Cricketer and explain my point of view.

To be fair to him, he tried calling The Cricketer multiple times, but to no avail. I remember him sending me a screengrab of his call records, which included at least four unanswered calls to The Cricketer. The Cricketer did not pick up, and the administrator could do little thereafter with a match on hand. He, however, promised to get in touch with me the following day, and make sure that the matter was sorted at the earliest. His plan was to set up a meeting between The Cricketer and myself at his house or at the Cricket Association of Bengal (CAB), and iron things out. That meeting, however, never took place. I never asked why.

There was one other member of the media fraternity in whom

I had confided, besides Kushan, and Arani, a respected and senior writer, and had worked for RevSportz in South Africa during the India tour in January 2022. We had been speaking for a while and were about to ink a long-term agreement. I remember him asking if it was me that The Cricketer was referring to. He wouldn't say a word in the public domain, but he needed to know. I told him everything that had happened, and asked if he would continue to work for RevSportz. To my relief, he agreed and said that he would cover Virat Kohli's 100th Test match for us, and that we should go ahead with the planning.

Things, however, changed the very next day. He sent me a text in the morning, saying that he needed to discuss something urgent. And when we got on a call, he said that while he was with me and understood what I was going through, he couldn't work for RevSportz anymore. This was apparently because someone in the establishment had told him that if he did so, he would be in trouble. For the cricket establishment, I was already persona non grata. With the pandemic and lockdowns already having caused big cuts in newsrooms, the journalist in question didn't want to put his career at risk. He said his father was over 70, and had been told by many of his golfing buddies that he shouldn't be seen working with someone who was a bully.

I understood where he was coming from, and we agreed to part ways. We have, however, been in touch subsequently, and he has always offered support.

Little did I know that this particular call was just the start of the downward spiral. It was around noon the same day that I got an email from the legal cell of one of RevSportz's sponsors.

The mail was extremely terse and humiliating. It said that on account of what had happened, the company no longer wished to associate with me or RevSportz. The contract was terminated with immediate effect. No explanation sought, no chances given. Interestingly, we still haven't been paid for the work done. There has been no communication since.

The same evening, February 21, Sharmistha and I decided to take stock. Could we continue with the company, for one sponsor walking out could well be a sign of things to come. We had 10 members in the team then, a number that has swelled to 37 now, and it was only fair that we called each one and took them into confidence. Each of them was present when the call asking for the interview was made to The Cricketer at 7:50 pm on February 13. They all knew the truth. I had shown them when the messages had been sent and told them why. I hoped that each one of them would stand by me. To my immense relief, they did. My first question to Sharmistha that evening was whether she was agreeable to sustaining the company using our family savings. There were salaries to pay, and overheads to take care of. If we did not have corporate support, it would mean using family monies to sustain the company. I was clear that our partners at RevSportz and strong pillars of support, shouldn't be asked to handle a crisis of my making. She, in return, asked a very simple question: Is it about money or is it about self-respect? 'If you say you haven't done anything wrong, shouldn't we continue with RevSportz, come what may?' she said. 'Is closing it down even an option? It is important for us to respond to this injustice in whatever way we can. If that means using all our savings, so be it.'

I was stunned. The words took time to sink in. I can now say that I wouldn't be writing this book if not for my family. The call had been taken, and we would continue. Despite all the online abuse and the insults, work had to go on. My friends asked me to stay off Twitter (now X) for a while and colleagues at Twitter (I then had a partnership with the platform) called to say they would inform me once the level of abuse had gone down. They wanted to keep the partnership with RevSportz on hold for a while, because it wasn't good optics to be associated with someone who had been labelled a bully.

Each time the abuse seemed to abate, some trigger or the other would give it oxygen. The Cricketer was commended by multiple media channels for being tight-lipped and not revealing my name in public. Perhaps it was missed that during these days when I was on the verge of a mental breakdown, he was on an interview-giving spree, and each interaction had a common thread. He hadn't named me because he was being deliberately considerate, but that didn't stop him wondering out loud why I didn't apologise. Did I not feel regret or remorse? While it apparently wasn't his intention to hurt someone's family, he declared that he had to put things out in the public domain so that no one would dare do such a thing to a cricketer in the future. His statements were predictably followed by a barrage of social media abuse and targeted insults from the trolls baying for my blood. It was enough to traumatise even the strongest. Interestingly, there was not one word from him, even without naming me, to allay this abuse being heaped on a journalist and his family. More so since most of the trolls also referred and mentioned him. While I was the primary target, my wife, daughter and parentage had all been dragged into it by the troll army. The Cricketer was conspicuously silent on that, even as he was being held up in the public eye as the victim. Here I ask, if he considered it his moral and social responsibility to bring out the improper nature of my WhatsApp messages to him on the night of the auction, what about one's moral and social awareness when violently abusive and psychologically damaging invectives are being hurled by a troll army, in the perspective of those very same revelations? Did he even once caution restraint to his followers? Urge them to allow the establishment or the Apex Body to decide on the matter? It could have been done, even without naming me, just like in the case of the allegations. It would have assuaged my wife, sister and mother.

If I remember right, it was in the fourth week of February that one of the office bearers of the Apex Body announced the setting up of a committee to probe the matter. He announced that The Cricketer would be urged to reveal his persecutor's name before the committee. My lawyers welcomed the news. It meant that I could also be asked to present my side of the story, because by law both sides need to be heard. What they hadn't taken into account was the power of trial by media. Hundreds of thousands of tweets, and hundreds of articles had already denounced me as a criminal. And when it was one person's word against another's, didn't a centrally contracted cricketer stand a better chance? He was one of their own, and how could I, an outsider, be believed when I claimed I had never threatened a cricketer? The supreme court of trolls had already pronounced me guilty and singled me out as worthy of a lynching, with even players of repute urging The Cricketer on social media to take a deep breath and reveal the name.

Before I go any further, it is important that I lay out the sequence of events, with respect to when the messages were sent and in what context. Did I send them immediately after The Cricketer was dropped from the Indian team? Was I implying that the interview I sought could save his place in the side, if he obliged me? Was I really so stupid? When it was public knowledge that the India coach had spoken to him in the dressing room and conveyed the decision that he would be dropped from the side, what further business did a journalist have in the matter? But then, what chance does logic have against the troll army?

And that is, in effect, a very grave reality of our times, not only in the case of myself, but such others as me who have been subjected to such online kangaroo courts.

In reality, the messages were sent on the night of February 13, within hours of The Cricketer being picked in the cricket league's auction.

I now turn to why and how this happened. A version I had also placed before the committee.

The dreaded messages

A week ahead of the auction, The Cricketer's manager and I planned to do interviews with a few of the players he managed. It would be good content for me ahead of the auction, and also help create some buzz around RevSportz. After all, the auction was the first after the inclusion of two new teams and would shape the future of the league. In October 2021, two new teams were added to the existing eight-team competition making it a ten-team extravaganza. New teams meant there had to be a mega auction for there had to be a realignment of players. For a new media company, it was a marquee event. Any content that I could generate would help.

On the basis of this plan, I interviewed Abdul Samad and Chetan Sakariya. Both these chats are on the RevSportz social-media platforms for all to see. The plan was also to interview The Cricketer, but with Krunal Pandya doing an interview with me on February 10, and Hardik Pandya, who had been appointed captain of a franchise, following his older brother, we couldn't find an appropriate slot ahead of the auction.

I needed a window to speak to The Cricketer, and the auction offered the best opportunity. On Day One, he went unsold, and each of us had felt bad for him. And it was only natural that the moment he was sold on Day Two, we would try and make use of the opportunity. He wasn't one of the auction headlines, and had we not spoken to him soon after he was sold, the news value would have been lost. Ishan Kishan and Shreyas Iyer were the two major stories coming out of the auction. Kishan had gone for 15.25 crores, while Iyer cost Kolkata Knight Riders 12.25 crores. As a media organisation, we had to focus on them in our auction review the next morning. We also had interviews lined up with Ashish Nehra and Gary Kirsten from one of the franchises, Gautam Gambhir from another of them, and two franchise owners. The next two days had looked choc-a-bloc.

We had done close to 20 interviews on the two auction days,

and by the time one of the franchises picked up The Cricketer, in the evening on the second day, my team was completely exhausted. We had worked tirelessly for a week, and each of us needed a break. Trisha Ghosal, who heads production for RevSportz, was adamant that we didn't need to speak to him. He wasn't important as a news point and we should just let things be, said Trisha. It was my voice that drowned her out, insisting that we support and profile a fellow Bengali. It was I that instructed Debasis Sen, one of my colleagues, to call The Cricketer within moments of him being selected. Debasis had known The Cricketer for years, and so had I. We had always been on friendly terms, something I will demonstrate with adequate proof in the next chapter. We shared a certain camaraderie and it was on that basis that Debasis, on my behalf, asked The Cricketer for a few minutes of his time. The Cricketer, for his part, told Debasis that he could do the interview at the Kalighat ground the following day. That's when I asked for Debasis's phone and made a personal request. My mother, 73, wasn't well, and with Covid still around, I did not want to go to the Kalighat ground and risk exposure.

While a face-to-face interview is always preferred, I was happy to forego that for a Zoom meeting because I did not want to take a chance. I therefore requested The Cricketer for a time that very evening, within the next hour or so, if that was possible. He told me that he was on his way home, and that if I sent him a Zoom link, he would do the interview within moments of reaching home. It was a warm conversation, and we generated the Zoom link soon after to send to him. With the chat fixed, I then requested a senior PR person, who was handling PR for one of the franchises, if I could talk to Kirsten a little later and if the Nehra interview, already fixed, could be pushed to the next day so that we could do justice to it. The said PR official, a lady who has always been helpful, readily agreed. I also called an official of another franchise, and asked if I could speak to the owner any time after 9:30 pm. My plan was to finish The Cricketer's interview, and then record with this franchise owner and Gary.

Anyone who is in the media business will tell you that each one of these interviews matters a lot on the day of an auction. This is the content that an organisation spreads out over the next few days. This bank of stories sustains momentum and keeps the platform buzzing. Each one of these conversations was important, and I was doubly careful to space them out so as to be able to do justice to each interview.

At 8 pm, I tried calling The Cricketer to check if he had reached home. He did not take the call, and I assumed that he was still en route. Thereafter, for the next hour and a half, we kept trying his numbers every 20 minutes or so. Debasis even remarked that he hoped things were okay, because it was unlike him to not respond. At 9 pm, the PR lady from one of the franchises called to ask if I was ready to speak to Gary. I was in two minds. What if The Cricketer called and wanted to do the interview? I had said to him I would do it, and I did not want him to think that I had opted for Gary because, as a former India coach, he was a bigger draw. As we waited, my team members were cursing me for wanting to do the interview. The Cricketer wasn't Hardik, and the interview wasn't going to go viral, so why was I still pushing everyone after two days of non-stop work? Things got a little heated, and when the official I had spoken to earlier called to say that we would have to reschedule the franchise owner's interview because he couldn't wait any longer, we let the frustration get to us. It was 9:30 pm by then, and we had all waited for an hour and a half. All that was needed was a message, telling us that The Cricketer couldn't do the interview or needed to postpone it to another day. That didn't happen. At 10 pm, I went ahead with the Kirsten interview, which had to be truncated to five minutes. We spoke to the two franchise owners thereafter, for we needed some content for the following day.

Each one of us felt let down. I was the one responsible, and it was natural that the team was upset with me for prolonging the workday. In my enthusiasm to focus on a player from Bengal, I had pushed everyone to keep going and also lost out on other key interviews which had been set up. We could easily have spoken to Nehra and Kirsten and got our headline. We could have spoken earlier to the two franchise owners, and had two other teams covered. Gautam Gambhir, mentor of another of the franchises, was again somebody who would always give you quotable answers. Why had I let all those opportunities slide by waiting two hours for The Cricketer to call? When I look back at what I did, I have to say I was stupid. That I had for a bit lost my sense of judgement. There was no reason for me to wait. I had tried to reach out to somebody I knew well and somebody that had promised the interview in the first place, but then hadn't responded. That should have been that.

The lack of any kind of response was what upset us the most, especially from one we considered a friend, and someone who had reached out to me for help quite a few times in the past—something I will elaborate in the next chapter.

One also needs to understand the nature of my relationship with The Cricketer at that point to comprehend why I kept calling. He wasn't Sakariya, who I had never spoken to before. He wasn't Samad, who I was introduced to for the first time. I had seen The Cricketer play for Bengal for years, and remembered his first press conference in Australia, for which he was an hour late. Australian journalists wanted to pounce on him for that tardiness and it was on us, the few Indians present, who stood up to protect him. We had even called each other, before a tour of West Indies, to fix haircut appointments, on the same day at the same time in the same salon, because he considered me lucky! And that is why I felt so let down. Angry. Frustrated. Why could he not have called or messaged and told me our chat wasn't happening? Why did I keep the team waiting and cancel multiple other interviews in the hope that he would pop up on the screen any moment?

When the team members finally went home at 10 pm, I went to my room completely drained and frustrated. It was then that I sent The Cricketer the texts that changed my life. On the night of the auction, when we had wanted to record an interview with him to celebrate a Bengal cricketer getting a contract. When a Zoom link that he had asked for had been sent well in advance.

One can certainly fault the language I used. But then again, the messages were sent in an emotional moment of heated frustration to somebody I had known for several years, and who had asked me for help in the past. Our interactions had a degree of comfort, and whatever I said was most certainly not a threat. I wasn't trying to bully The Cricketer, nor was I implying that I would *or even that I could* harm his chances of playing for India if he didn't agree to the interview. The very suggestion is outrageous. His Test career was in no way connected to my messages, but his own performance as with any other player. The Cricketer, the Indian team management, and dozens of others know as much. So, to be told that I tried to threaten him on the ground of not securing an interview, or that I had any intentions or even the ability to finish his career was to me like a body blow.

As for my claim that he should speak to the best, and speak to me first, that should hardly raise an eyebrow in any newsroom. Go to any editor or journalist worth his or her salt, and check if they haven't asked for an exclusive and the privilege of getting it first. If someone says that he or she hasn't, all I will say is that it's a bare-faced lie. Each of us wants our exclusives, because our professional standing depends on it, and we all want to be the one to get it first. That's the nature of the game. The media has forever operated like that. Otherwise, the news ecosystem would be run only on press releases. An interview is granted to someone who can make it worth the trouble. Would the Prime Minister or Home Minister or any other senior politician speak to any and every journalist? Why do only some newsmakers get to speak to them? Does every media house get the same number of exclusives? And why do then top media houses play up these very same exclusives? Does any journalist of repute pass on the chance of an exclusive with someone they know well? Was suggesting that it was worth The Cricketer's time to speak to me worthy of a two-year ban? Also, while it was most certainly The Cricketer's prerogative and a matter of his free will to give me the interview, as it should be with any athlete, there are also codes of conduct that require calls and messages to be returned if you have *actually* promised that interview to somebody, if even to say that you are subsequently unable to do the same interview. I have team members who are ready to publicly acknowledge that The Cricketer *did agree* to the zoom interview once he returned home that night. I have worked with the world's top cricketers, been biographer to one of India's all-time great cricketers, and interviewed top international athletes in all disciplines and sports. Yet, very seldom have I encountered such a dismissive and disrespectful attitude towards the members of my profession from a player or athlete as was displayed the night of the auction by The Cricketer towards myself and my entire team. A profession called journalism, whose members toil night and day to bring coverage of players and athletes to people at large, and celebrate them. I had tried to convey this anguish to the esteemed committee.

But, by then, the kangaroo court of trolls, which feasts on hatred and social media negativity, had already declared my guilt, and trolls were my jury. When a story acquires a life of its own on Twitter or Instagram, committees like the one set up by the Apex Body find themselves confronted with this toxic tide of 'public opinion'. And that is where I raise another crucial question, which is much larger than myself or what my own family has suffered. Should responsible public personalities with social media followings splash their personal grievances on such volatile social media platforms knowing full well that a public spectacle will ensue? Or should they be more responsible and discreet if even they wish to bring attention to their grievances? If The Cricketer felt so outraged by my messages to him on the night of the auction why did he not inform the sport's Apex Body in the country (which anyway eventually formed a committee to address the issue) through email or other direct means? Why did he, on the one hand, refuse to divulge my name when the Apex Body first contacted him on the matter through email, and then, on the same day, post again, on the very same social media platform stating he had been hurt, offended and did not wish anybody else to be bullied? After his second tweet, the tide of abuse against me was re-ignited. If the same abuse had shown any signs of abating since the first tweet, it multiplied after this second tweet by The Cricketer. ***This abuse would not be allowed to settle,*** I realised.

Somebody could make the case that The Cricketer himself cannot be held responsible for online abuse directed at somebody. After all, he himself had not instructed anybody to roll out this kind of abuse. Once again, public personalities with celebrity stature and corresponding social media followings do know full well how such platforms function, or can be made to respond to certain kinds of postings. Children can well plead unawareness of the consequences of their actions, not responsible professionals who are also respected public personalities.

Why was a public spectacle necessary (made all the more spectacular by the fact that it initially involved a guessing game on social media about the journalist's identity), one which went on to unleash abuse and vitriol that traumatised my mother and sister, and made my wife the target of bullying on social media? That's right, even my own were a target of bullying and intimidation. Why was this very public outcry of victimhood necessary, and on that particular and fateful evening? And not on any of the five other days that followed the day of the messages being sent. It is a question that needs to be asked repeatedly in this matter, and one that became submerged in the avalanche of social media diatribe. The Cricketer had apparently refused to reveal or state my name in public ON GROUNDS OF HUMANITY. I now ask this question, where went that same humanity when I was dehumanised in public, day after day, and months on end, even after my ban was in place. Did it take much to know that I too had a family and that they too could be intimidated and traumatised?

I have alluded at various times to The Cricketer seeking my help in the past, and the cordial relationship that we had shared. It is important I prove that, else I could be accused of lying again. This time, I will draw upon (without directly reproducing them as that could amount to a breach of privacy) personal WhatsApp messages that he had sent to me.

3

The Cricketer and Me

In the two days after The Cricketer put out his tweet, social media vilification reached a peak. The instant justice brigade wrote and rewrote the abuse. The more extreme posts wanted me lynched or even jailed. Each such tweet got hundreds of likes, and seemed to increase the mob's bloodlust. It was public shaming of a kind I had not seen before—the equivalent of burning someone's effigy for days. Those that wanted the most attention tended to post their comments on The Cricketer's timeline, as a response to his original tweet. There seemed to be a competition on, to see who could frame the most abusive message. Having my name dragged through the online sewer wasn't enough. I needed to be crushed and broken, and memes won the day as the weapon of choice.

Two examples illustrated this best. One tweet, posted as a response to The Cricketer's original one, had the picture of a dog on a leash. The dog looked scared and had turned its face away, as though it had done something seriously wrong and had been reprimanded for it. That was supposed to be me. The leash was instructive to say the least. I needed to be tamed and taught a lesson.

First things first. I'm not irked in the slightest by being compared to a dog. They are the most amazing companions, and far more loyal than many human beings. Also, dogs don't indulge in lies and deceit. I have loved dogs since I was a boy, and was heartbroken to lose two of them in the same year as this incident. The gentleman in question—a self-styled social-media influencer—perhaps lacked the sensitivity to understand just how much a dog can mean to many of us. Maybe the said abuser thought he would look like a big man when he put out that tweet.

A second tweet had a picture of a different dog. Only in this case, it was clearly labelled—'He'. In that image, the dog was looking at the camera with its eyes and ears down. It had its two front paws in a folded position, as if asking forgiveness for a crime committed.

I have just described two of over 200,000 tweets. Neither was an aberration. They were very much the norm. The Cricketer, the morally upright soul who did not wish to hurt my family or I, offered not a single response or rebuke. The most vicious tweets were almost all on his timeline, as responses to his first message. Was this spectacle actually serving to advance anybody's purpose? Some might want to give The Cricketer a benefit of doubt and say that he may not have seen these abusive tweets on his timeline. Seriously? After a tweet like that setting alight a fire of controversy, wouldn't anybody have checked the reactions? The fact of the matter remains that not a finger was raised to stop or condemn the barrage of abuse. Some words of caution, without my name being taken, might have brought a bit of sanity even as the controversy ran its course. If many of them were his fans and well-wishers perhaps they would have listened to a reasoned voice. But, if anything, the abuse actually spiralled when he declared in interview after interview thereafter that he was forced to go public because there had been no apology or remorse from my side. He also stated that I had always pressured him with my pushy and aggressive behaviour.

I have just two questions for The Cricketer.

If he had always found my tone and attitude so offensive, why did he reach out to me in mid-2018, when he was doing his rehab at the National Cricket Academy (NCA) after a serious injury? That was in the middle of a very long spell where he didn't play for India, when he looked finished as an international cricketer. I have quoted from those WhatsApp messages in this chapter, as they were received.

Secondly, he was The Cricketer who had represented India in many Tests spread across more than a decade. He was not some wet-behind-the-ears Under-19 kid to be intimidated by me or anyone else. Why did he tolerate such allegedly reprehensible behaviour for so long? Why would he pose with my books and post those images on his social media platforms? For the record, I never paid him a single penny to do so. He did so of his own *prerogative* and his *free will*. From my side, I invited him to several shows I did for television because I considered him a cricketer of distinction, whose career I had followed for more than a decade. If he had felt threatened, he could have asked me to take a hike much earlier. Blocked my number. Why promote my books, or respond to my messages or engage with me on social media?

I come from a family of distinguished physicians. Both my father and grandfather made their names by healing people. The idea that I could somehow intimidate and traumatise The Cricketer and his family—or that I could be a maker and breaker of fortunes in Indian cricket—was as laughable as it was preposterous.

Less than two years before the incident, towards the end of 2020, The Cricketer had appeared on a show of mine with two other cricketers. Afterwards, he tweeted: 'Thank you for having me _____-da. Loved the chat session with you.'

Another tweet from a year earlier, dated November 28, 2019, reads: 'Excited about the #Inspiration series on _____(the television network I then worked for) Looking forward to watch this one.' I responded, saying, '_____ get well soon and look forward to your feedback. Thank you.'

'Thank you _____-da,' said his subsequent response. 'Your show will be a blockbuster. My best wishes as always.' I had asked him to watch the show, and valued his feedback. I did so because I had good relations with him.

What do these tweets tell you? Do they seem to have been made under duress? Why wish me the best for a show that he wasn't even a part of? Yet, just over two years later, the same Cricketer who asserted that my show would be a massive hit had no hesitation in calling me a bully, *and moreover that I had been intimidating him for the past several years.* It ended in seriously damaging my career and reputation. So, what changed?

There are two parts to the answer. When The Cricketer was dropped from the Indian team in February 2022, his response was to publicly vent, on a social media platform, against the national coach, and a top office bearer of the Apex Body. Few athletes, in any sphere of sporting endeavour, could hope to get away with such public comments and conduct. Did he then realise that he had consequences to face? Did he possibly think that he needed to deflect attention away from his indiscretion to something else?

And since he was no longer part of the national set-up, had I actually outlived my usefulness as an ally in the media? My relationship with the cricketing legend whose biographer I am fortunate enough to be—just one example—endures a decade after we did his autobiography together. It isn't based on 'What can I get out of this?' Real relationships endure, others fall apart or are ripped apart. My relations with The Cricketer were ripped apart. And through the entire period of the controversy my hard-earned reputation in my field of work was mercilessly trampled.

You talk to any sportsperson, and they will tell you that the dressing room is a sacred space. What happens there is not for public consumption. The same goes for conversations that the coach and an office bearer of the Apex Body have had with you regarding the future of your cricketing career. By going public with details of those private conversations on a social media platform, a code of conduct is shattered. Possibly, it was anticipated that there would be a heavy price to pay. A smokescreen was a way out.

To say things to a committee behind closed doors, when you know you won't be cross-examined, is easy. Had I been given the right to respond to the allegations in the same space, I would have countered them in minutes. But since I couldn't directly counter, shredding my reputation was as easy as putting away a wide half-volley. In the court of public opinion, The Cricketer was anyway the victim.

As I look back on the course of events that unfolded to brand me a bully, some statements made by The Cricketer before the committee (and now in the public domain) stand out for their melodramatic quality. He said he was unable to leave his home in the city where we both live without fear and apprehension. That he had felt unsafe travelling to the airport in his own vehicle and chose a different car, ostensibly for fear of identification. By me? To say the least, professionals like me don't run spy agencies and some things are best left for the 007 franchise.

Through the time during the last two years that I have battled disrepute, my wife and I ensured that our only daughter—while she must have sensed our helplessness and despondency at times—was largely allowed to grow carefree and with a sense of security. We consider it an achievement that we were able to safeguard her against the hate that we ourselves encountered. Can The Cricketer even fathom that my own family came close to the point of a breakdown on account of the hatred that we encountered? I hope that any parent who reads this account appreciates how much it took for me to keep up a brave front for the sake of my child. It is *my child* that might easily have been traumatised in those circumstances, like *my sister*, a cancer survivor, and *my mother* had effectively become anxious, perturbed and traumatised. I am also thankful that my daughter was only eight then and not thirteen or fourteen, and not on social media herself to witness her father's humiliation and utter degradation.

The past

I had known The Cricketer from the time he made his Test debut. It wasn't a memorable debut. He was out for a duck in the first innings. In the second dig, though, he showed pluck against a fiery pace attack. India lost by an innings, and he was dropped from the squad for the next Test. For the immediate future, that was that.

I was covering that game, and remember speaking to him after it was over. At the time, he did not seem comfortable speaking to the media, but he opened up on how tough it had been to step in at the last minute. Conversing in Bangla helped, and he looked pleased to be able to confide in someone who spoke his language. He said some things which were best not said to a newly made acquaintance about the establishment, and would have made juicy headlines. But this was a young man trying his best to cut his teeth in international cricket. And I did not write a line on any of it.

The Cricketer got his next opportunity in Test cricket nearly two years later. It was one of Indian cricket's biggest misadventures, and India would lose eight overseas Test matches on the trot in the course of the next seven months.

During that same test series, with senior players unwilling to face the media, The Cricketer was sent on one occasion to address a press conference, the first time he had done so at the international level. It was originally scheduled around lunch time, but due to some miscommunication, he and the Indian team manager turned up an hour late. The Australian journalists, understandably, were livid. The travelling Indian media corps weren't best pleased either. Everyone was restless and appalled by the apparently unprofessional attitude. The start of the interaction was rough, with The Cricketer being asked a number of unpleasant questions. He was in the line of fire but the time of the press conference communicated to him had been incorrect. Once he explained as much to a few of us in Bangla, we did our best to step up for him. And he seemed relieved that things settled down thereafter.

That was the start of our association. Thereafter, I attended a number of his Ranji Trophy games, and our relationship grew over time. While we were never very close, there was always mutual respect. Or so I assumed!

The relations became stronger in 2017-18. But before I detail some of our exchanges from that time, I would like to digress and point the reader towards an op-ed I wrote about The Cricketer for a Bengali daily towards the end of 2021. This is an essence of what I had then written:

If you happen to meet him at any point in Kolkata, you will inevitably hear him say, '_____-da, how are you? How are things at home? How is your daughter?' Completely focussed on the job at hand, he very seldom speaks much. In fact, if my readers ask me, I would say he should speak a bit more. He must invest a bit more on getting his brand across to more people. Be a little more active perhaps on social media. All he wants to do is play cricket. Having scored a spectacular fifty…braving injury, he followed it up…with yet another crucial innings at a time when India needed it the most… he had to be patient and yet play his shots from the very start. And he did…and his innings could go a long way in setting the match up for India.

In the Cricket League too, we have seen him play some very similar impactful innings. Much to the surprise of many, he has come out all guns blazing…

So, how good is he? While many have complained about the lack of runs in the past, a former fielding coach is all praise for his work ethic, arguing that he is still trying to be perfect. And also that the same is what sets him apart, the hallmark of a good cricketer.

You ask The Cricketer, and he will say, 'I am not doing anything different, to be honest. I just focus on the ball till the very last second, and commit to what I am doing. There is no point in complicating things. If you keep your technique simple, you will get your rewards.'

The last two years have been tough on him. Multiple injuries have laid him low… However, it doesn't bother him. A perfect team player, he is very much at peace with himself. I remember we were both getting haircuts in the same salon in Kolkata the day before he left for an important tour, and I asked him this question. 'Do you feel apprehensive?' All he said was, 'I will give it my best if the opportunity arises. I have always tried to control things that are in my hands. What isn't controllable should just be left alone. It is not in my hands to get picked in the first eleven. You can't get frustrated if you are not picked. You have to keep working hard, and wait for your turn. And once you are given an opportunity, just try and make the most of it. While I was out with an injury, at no point did I ever give up or feel I wouldn't be able to come back. I never lost focus, that's for sure.'

For Indian cricket, we want him to not lose focus, for, in the process, he could well help the country win some more important matches. With the volume of cricket being played going back to the old normal, and more, there is little doubt that he will get his opportunities. And he needs to be ready to continuously remind the world how good he is. And then, it is on us. The media. We need to stay true, and back the man. More so in Bengal. He is one of our own, and needs the support that we can offer him. We need to keep talking and writing about him to ensure that he is there or thereabouts always. With the Cricket League auction coming up, it is pertinent to showcase the knocks he has played in the League in the last couple of seasons. Not being flamboyant shouldn't go against a talented man, and it is absolutely imperative we ensure that. Not being flashy isn't something to lose sleep over. Not making controversial statements shouldn't be seen as timidity. He is how he is. Solid and reliable. And that's what we need to sell and market. Go well, _The Cricketer_.

Having written such a piece about him 55 days before our relationship was destroyed, it was unreal for me to be told that I had been intimidating or pressuring him for 2-3 years preceding his tweets (as he claimed before the committee). The editor of the page could tell you that there was no pressure on me to write what I wrote. I chose the subjects that I wrote about. No one ever said to me that I needed to write about The Cricketer. I sincerely believed that he needed to be backed. And I did so without knowing that he found me aggressive and disliked talking to me, as he claimed in front of the committee. He should certainly have told me so personally. And I would have respected it and kept my distance from him.

Long before the above referenced op-ed for the Bengali daily, I had done an interview of him for a national newspaper, published in November, 2019. The Cricketer had then tweeted the link to the interview, with the following words: '*It is always a delight to talk to Boria da.* Here's my interview with him for ____. Read the full interview at...'

I have reproduced the tweet in the images section. What is instructive is the tone of his tweet. I leave it to the readers to judge if it was celebratory or not. Was it not basking in the glory of the media spotlight? If I was *always* aggressive, as he subsequently claimed, did it make any sense for him to tweet what he did then? I most certainly did not coerce him to tweet out my article. Either I constantly pushed him around, and he hated that, or he enjoyed speaking to me, and me writing about him. It simply couldn't have been both, and therein his claim that he had felt pressured by me for the past 2-3 years and that I had always been aggressive with him needed re-examination. Each of those posts is still there on his timeline, as this book goes to press.

This wasn't the only interview of The Cricketer I did for the same national daily. I interviewed him again for the very same newspaper towards the end of 2021, and the introduction to the interview was as follows. '*Many had written him off... And yet he came roaring back...braving pain... It was an innings of quality and one that went a long way in winning India the match and the series. Currently in Kolkata for a couple of days…he spoke about the forthcoming…series, questions around his batting, battling injury… and more.'*

It was a detailed interview, which had aimed to give The Cricketer his due and celebrate his achievements in the recently concluded series. In the very same way that I had intended to do after the cricket league's auction of February 13, days before he tweeted against me.

Against the backdrop of all these interactions, the notion that I had tried to harm him and was always intimidating was an assault on my integrity. But in the hands of social media trolls with superfluous agendas, fiction can very easily be passed for fact.

Clinching evidence

In mid-2018, *The Hindustan Times* published a news report which detailed The Cricketer's successive injuries which he had suffered since the start of that year, and also that he was expected to be out of action for some more months on account of a surgery.

There are two key points in that copy. With multiple injuries impacting his career, The Cricketer had sat out more games than he had played that year. Second, and far more important, was the assertion that his rehab at the NCA had not been as it should. This wasn't the only report that said so, and anyone who covered Indian cricket at the time would testify that this was the perception that had gained ground.

A couple of weeks before the report was published, I had

reached out to The Cricketer, offering support in any way needed. Later, we exchanged a few messages. The WhatsApp conversation, from which I have quoted below exactly as it happened, is self-explanatory.

Wed, 18 Jul

Boria
******** do you need any help

Boria
Just know I am a call away

Boria
Feel free to call anytime

Boria
Whatever support I can give I will for you

Boria
Please note this is when friends come to the fore

Boria
And I will be with you more in bad than in good.

The Cricketer
Ok I will let you know if I need anything.

Boria
Just a call away

The Cricketer
Thumbs up.

Fri, 20 Jul

Boria
How bad is it (the shoulder)

The Cricketer
Operation korate hobe (I will have to get it operated upon)

(It should be noted here that I was aware of the surgery two weeks before it happened. If I wanted to, I could easily have done a news story.)

Boria
Bloody F

Boria
How long will the recovery time be?

The Cricketer
Seta doc bolte parbe (That the doctors can say)

Boria
Will you be ready for Australia? When is the operation and where? Holo ki kore? (How did it happen?)

The Cricketer
If fit before that then surely

The Cricketer
In nxt 7/10 days in UK

Boria
I am going on August 5

Boria
Let me know where you will be

Boria
And if you need anything

The Cricketer
Ok will let you know.

Boria
Holo ki kore (How did it happen)

The Cricketer
...series theke ferar por thn ipl e dive (After the series, after I returned...then I dived during the IPL)

Boria
So operation is a must?

The Cricketer
Day by day kharap hochhe operate na korale (It is going from bad to worse by the day if I don't get it operated upon)

Boria
Kore nao ____ (Get it done ____)

Boria
India needs you. And imp for your career also.

The Cricketer
(The folded hands emoji)

Boria
Don't let others take the spot. I am with you always.

The Cricketer
Thanks. (And a smiley)

The conversation above was clearly a conversation between two people known well to each other, and I did not intend to write about it. The Cricketer however, wrote to me again the same day, and I gauged a request to write about his situation without naming him.

The Cricketer
Ami bolechi erom likho na (Don't write that I told you)

The Cricketer
Jante perecho seta likho (That you have come to know, *write that*)

The Cricketer
Karon ja hochhe dekchi (Because of what all I am seeing happening around me)

Boria
Exactly

Boria
I will just state the facts

The Cricketer
Ok

While there were many more messages exchanged between 2018 and 2021, the only noteworthy aspect of those chats is that we were two fellows who trusted each other. Why else would The Cricketer message me, 'Don't write that I told you. That you have come to know, write that.'

If I had been persistently bullying or pressuring him, would this exchange have taken place? He was out of the team at the time, and far from headline material. If I'm being cynical, from a news standpoint, I had nothing to gain by talking to him. I exchanged a few messages with a cricketer who had almost become a friend, and who I imagined needed some positive reinforcement because things had not gone according to plan.

To then get to know that he had said what he did in front of the committee was a shock. Does the exchange I have detailed suggest any aggression on my part? Is there a hint of a threat? We bumped into each other multiple times at the AN John Hair Salon on Park Street in Kolkata, where both of us went for our haircuts. During one of our interactions there, The Cricketer joked that we should coordinate our haircuts in the future, for I was lucky for him. It was just before a tour to the West Indies to put it on record. Although we both laughed at the suggestion, sport involves so many superstitions that neither of us dismissed it.

As I finish this chapter, and after going through all our past interactions and the pieces and interviews I had done on/with The Cricketer—including one just two months before the incident—I ask my readers to think through what might have prompted The Cricketer to act in the manner that he did. After an association that went back more than a decade, was it his sole disaffection with my messages of February 13? Why did he not call and speak to me? Or message saying they had hurt or annoyed him? What was worth tweeting out those messages that ended in damaging my career and disrupting my life? And why was that optics relevant on that very same day when he was dropped from the national team? These are questions that need to be thought through.

I can think of no greater irony than the fact that, for over a decade, I wrote of The Cricketer being an almost shy and uncontroversial individual who didn't get the attention that his more flashy or flamboyant peers did. With one tweet, he showed me just what a bad judge of character I had been.

Many, including my RevSportz colleagues, have asked why did I not sit down with some of the people I knew well and had worked with over the years, and tell them what really had happened—my version, which few knew. Couldn't I have asked them why they responded with such indifference when I needed their support the most? Paji as he is fondly called, for example, was a good friend with whom I shared some of my best moments during our stints at the previous news channel where I had worked, both of us leading sport. Why would someone as senior as him give a miss to my side of the story? When he knew me well enough to call me in the middle of the night. Perhaps he wasn't aware that somebody who worked directly under him had called my RevSportz colleague, repeatedly coaxing him to speak against me? But then, he surely knew that his own channel had done several stories on the issue, without once asking for my version of things. Could he not have called me personally? As a friend and cohort, if nothing else. For if one journalist could face a social media trial today, another could be facing it tomorrow, and didn't we then need to stand with each other?

I could have asked him in Australia when we were both covering the T20 World Cup (2022), and again in England during the WTC final (2023). I could have taken Paji out for a coffee, and asked him those questions. I could have asked the same questions of the journalist that had called my RevSportz colleague to speak against me. The truth is that I did not want to, during those times. I needed to endure this ban and the pain and the trauma before I put out my story. Each day has been a torment. To live with the charges, and be called a bully by every Johnny Come Lately on social media, hasn't been easy. I came close to consulting a therapist on several occasions. But I managed to get through it all for my family and friends.

Now, through this book, let me ask my old colleague those questions which I did not ask then. Sometimes even after a storm, equations stay unchanged as is the case between me and one of India's greatest off-spinners. He had tweeted about the incident when it had come to light, but when told by a common friend who The Cricketer's tweet was directed at, he had apparently informed that he had no idea it was about me. He told the friend in question that he knew me well and there must have been something more to it than what came out. Since then, we have met multiple times, and he has treated me no differently than before the incident. On the face of it I could say the same for some of my ex-colleagues who I have met and interacted with on several occasions since the ban, and who have been warm enough.

Going forward, will I hold anything against my ex-colleague or some others for not reaching out for my side of the story? The truth is I probably would have, had I not written this book. The book is my closure. Now, I can call Paji and request him to read it. He can join me for a cup of coffee, and then invite me on his show if he so wishes. His viewers, and they number in millions, need to know my side of the story. After the years we spent working together, I hope we have that little mojo still remaining between us.

4

The Verdict and the Aftermath

Just imagine being told that you will be shot one day. The date hasn't been decided, and you don't know whether you'll survive. All you do know is that you face the firing squad for something that you did not do. A crime that was a figment of someone's imagination, but no one was prepared to listen to you because it had already become Gospel truth for social media. That was the state of limbo I found myself in for two months.

Between February 20 and April 23, 2022, when the Apex Body met to impose a two-year sanction on me, not a single day passed without someone calling me to hint at dire consequences. Some suggested that the Apex Body would take cognisance of my contribution over the past 20 years and merely issue a caution. Others thought I could be banned for life. Another group thought I should go back to academia, and leave behind the rather politicised sports-media domain. None of this made any sense.

As a journalist, I had only done my job in following up about an interview that had already been arranged. Yes, I had sent The Cricketer a message in my frustration but it had been an emotional outburst. Haven't each one of us done that, sometime or another? How did telling somebody I wouldn't interview him again because he had held me up, or that I felt insulted on account of his behaviour, amount to *threatening* him? But the steady stream of words and innuendo acted like slow poison. I was desperate to tell my side of the story, but no one was prepared to give it any credence.

At one level, I prayed that whatever the outcome, it should happen fast. At least clarity would allow me to recalibrate and move on. My lawyers, and I had consulted a slew of senior ones at the time, had all told me that if I moved court, there was a good chance I would get a stay order. The date on my messages had been blurred out before being posted on social media, and couldn't be used as admissible evidence. It was also a breach of my privacy for somebody to put out personal WhatsApp chats without my consent—that's how the law defines it. I had a pretty strong case. Some advised me to pursue a defamation case against The Cricketer. I considered that seriously, and even paid the fees at the Calcutta High Court.

My fight was never against the Apex Body. The Apex Body was hearing out a centrally contracted cricketer who claimed to have been mistreated by a journalist. To start off, they had no mechanisms in place to verify who was speaking the truth.

In case I had gone down the legal route, it would have meant a protracted tussle that the Apex Body would also have been part of. That made no sense. Had The Cricketer not been a centrally contracted player, and had it only been a case of one man's word against another's, it would have been a different matter.

Therefore, once we decided to walk away from that path, despite having already invested much time and money into legal and court fees, the only option left was to wait for the verdict. I had met the committee set up by the Apex Body in March 2022, and presented my side of the story. The meeting, which was recorded, lasted for an hour and a half and each of the committee members heard me patiently. I couldn't have been clearer—I had not threatened anybody, it was my messages that had been taken out of context to create a social media spectacle. I told them that I believed that my messages had been used in the context of the announcement of the Test squad to effectively garner immense public sympathy, support and limelight.

Let's face facts here. In a normal news week, The Cricketer being dropped from the squad would have been a footnote at best. It certainly wouldn't have warranted trending hashtags on Twitter or long debates on prime-time television. But once flagged as a victim, ostensibly of intimidation by a well-known journalist, he migrated from a one-column news item on the inner pages to banner headlines on the front and back of newspapers...possibly with a hope of resurrection by dint of a popular consensus.

I did what I had to before the committee. I told them my truth. But, by then my guilt had been carved in stone on social media. To be fair to the committee, they also felt that the abuse heaped on my family was outrageous, and they told me as much several times during the meeting. And the Chairman has said so many times to me since.

After that hearing in March, I had no idea how long they would take to arrive at a decision. Finally, on April 12, Kushan called me to say that the item was on the agenda for the Apex Body's meeting of April 23. I was on close personal terms with a top office bearer of the Apex Body—for the last two decades we have been friends though thick and thin—and many believed I would use this proximity to him to try and influence the outcome. However, the truth is that on this topic, I had next to no interaction with him.

While I still believed that he believed my truth, I didn't expect him to swim against the tide on my behalf. One of the members of the committee that investigated the issue, had also known me for over 20 years and we still share a very warm relationship. In fact, we had a long conversation during the WTC final at The Oval, and I understood what he must have gone through, personally, sitting there in judgement over a friend. It was The Cricketer's allegation against my word. I won't deny that I felt devastated at the time. My reputation had been severely damaged and my very livelihood put at risk.

Going back to April 23, I was anxious to know what was going on. As a journalist, it was second nature to call sources to find out more about a developing story. But that day, I did nothing of the sort. Because, this time, I was the subject and not the reporter. Eventually, at 7 pm, Kushan sent me a message, saying that I had been banned for two years.

If you've been punched in the gut, you'll know how I felt right then. The sanction was far harsher than I had imagined, and to my mind, blatantly unfair. If I didn't believe that, I wouldn't have written this book.

At the time though, I was more concerned about the fallout from the ban on RevSportz. There was a team in place, which couldn't be impacted by an issue that only I was part of. Protecting them was my priority. There was euphoria on Twitter soon after the ban was announced. It had taken the kangaroo court just two months to get the verdict they wanted. I was also well aware that fellow journalists had lobbied relentlessly to have me pushed out of the grid. The ban meant that I could not work or generate stories in the field of cricket, and it was a jubilation for those that saw me as their worst competition. The Cricketer's agenda, whatever that was, had prevailed. But with my family and friends by my side, I wasn't about to go quietly. For the past two years I have seen messages, almost all abusive, which say that I haven't apologised and I feel no remorse for my actions. They're right. And this book explains why.

I remember going to bed that night thinking I should consult my lawyers again regarding the legal option. But once the initial dismay and sadness had subsided, I decided to move forward. Unlike John Osborne's character from the famous play, I couldn't afford to look back in anger. After being submitted to every sort of indignity for two months, I needed closure—for that moment. The bullets had been fired, and I was still standing.

The next morning, I woke up feeling almost at peace. The uncertainty was behind me. For the trolls, the ban was a full stop. For me, it was the first chapter in a new story, one I had to tell to clear my name. The phone wouldn't stop ringing, and I don't remember everyone that called. I do remember that there were a few missed calls from Kushan, among several hundred, and another from a journalist I knew. I have kept the messages and gone through them a dozen times during the course of writing this book. Kushan was one of the few who stayed with me through the crisis, and he continues to be one of my closest friends. He knew every detail, and was the one who had kept me informed on all developments. And yet, there was a message from him asking me to react to the verdict.

I felt disappointed and let down. Why would he send me such a message? When you have just been handed a two-year sanction for something you didn't do, what could your reaction possibly be? Whatever I said would only have added to the vitriol. I chose to stay silent and absorb all that was happening around me. Kushan and I did have a long chat a few days later, and the first thing he did was apologise. As a journalist, it was his job to ask for my reaction. He understood that it wasn't the sensitive or considerate thing to do, and said as much to me. I knew that he shared my pain and was sincere. We moved on, and our bond has only grown stronger.

The day after the ban was announced, a top functionary of the Apex Body called me to meet with him. I knew why. As an old friend, he felt bad, and we needed to meet and clear the air. Contrary to popular perception, we met only once in the two months between February 20 and April 23—a meeting that was reported in the media as being part of some secret plan. The entire issue had caused considerable unease. Whatever could I have said to him? That I wasn't at fault and that, as a functionary of the Apex Body he should believe my side of the story and do whatever he could? Even friendships have their boundaries, and at the end of every day it is each to his own. Even the best-meaning friends and supporters are sometimes left powerless when the tide and time is against you. The circumstances that I had passed through had left me with that realisation.

Instead, when we met on April 24, he told me: 'No one can stop you if you are honest and continue to work hard.' Those words stayed with me. The person in question has since moved on from the Apex Body, and when I look back, I'm proud that he did not wield any influence to try and save me. Had he persuaded or prevailed upon the Apex Body to not take any action, both of us would have been branded for life—he for misuse of power, and I as the culprit who benefited from his proximity to that power. And oh so ironically, it proved that I clearly wasn't so powerful as had been projected by The Cricketer. Not so powerful as to make anybody feel so threatened, no matter what they claimed and had put out to the world, nor powerful enough to decide the futures of cricketers. I had absolutely no ability or position whatsoever to influence the dropping of any cricketer from any side, Test or league cricket, as had been peddled on social media. I did not even manage to save myself and my family from public humiliation and trauma, and my company from financial loss, which it suffered on account of the social media trial that I was subjected to.

The naysayers still won't care for my side of the story. But the one thing they can't say is that I used my connections to escape the consequences of my alleged actions. I served my ban and suffered for 730 days. Lived with the ignominy of being labelled a bully. During these months, which I treated like a test, I did work that I am now immensely proud of and learned things that I did not know were possible. RevSportz has grown exponentially, and our sponsors have stuck with us to make the platform stronger than ever. Towards them, my gratitude is immense.

While I had always covered multiple sports, cricket was the prime focus. Having studied the sport for a doctoral degree, that was but natural. But now, I had been pushed out of my comfort zone, and I had to find other avenues. Even RevSportz needed a new path, and those are always challenging. Would the ban impact my relationship with other sports federations as well? With international sporting bodies? With players who were close friends and had been for years? Could I continue to work with the same passion, or would this entire bitter and traumatic experience make me cynical?

The cricket league was going on at the time, and whatever I tweeted was met with torrents of abuse. I needed a break to get my bearings back. So I did what was almost second nature by then, and what I did every year anyway—I left for Oxford. I had learned a lot in that city and, in a sense, identified with it. While no one knew me there, I knew every bit of it. I could wake up and not have to read the sports pages in the Bengali newspapers. I needed to put a distance between that episode and myself. In Oxford, the cricket league had no presence, it wouldn't be on every evening on television, and my phone wouldn't ring every few minutes. I could sit in the University Parks and think of what I now needed to do. Having my family with me meant that each time I felt low and crushed by what had happened, I could just be myself without the fear of being misunderstood. I could take my daughter to the bookshops we both loved and just watch her grow. Somehow I wanted her to grow up fast at that time, to only be able to tell her everything I had gone through.

It was a good time to leave too because there was no ambiguity about the ban. The announcement had been carried by the media, and there were several follow-up articles. Between April 23, 2022 and April 22, 2024, I wouldn't be allowed to go to grounds in India, or be able to speak to contracted cricketers. Interviews were out of the question. The Cricketer's allegations and his actions on social media took away my calling card. But sport was my life. Neither he, nor anyone else, could take that away from me. His doings had already inflicted untold damage on my family, and I knew that things could not get any worse. Possibly it was the lowest low for me, and things could now only look up.

Oxford—Where it all began

The link with Oxford went back nearly 25 years. I was awarded the Rhodes scholarship in 1999-2000, to do a D.Phil. on the social history of Indian cricket, and left for Oxford on September 30, 2000. Little did I know that it was the last time I would see my father. Prodosh Majumdar was an excellent and well-respected doctor—our family introduced homeopathy to India, and there is even a street named in honour of that contribution in Kolkata. My father was the last in the line of those doctors, but for me, he was another loved one I was leaving behind as I pursued my dream.

On our way to the airport, after I realised that I had left my belt at home, we stopped so that he could buy me another. That was his last gift to me. As we said our goodbyes, he asked me to call home once I had reached college and had settled in. I did call, but he wasn't there anymore. Even before my first day in Oxford was over, I got the news that my father had suffered a cardiac arrest. There was a note stuck to my room door, asking me to call India, and saying that it was urgent. I rushed to the porters' lodge, where I was told that I had lost my father and should call home immediately.

He was just 57 years old. My mother and sister never had the chance to move him to a hospital or nursing home. Coming back to India by the first available flight, thanks to the generosity of the Rhodes Trust, I knew that things would never be the same. I returned to Oxford four months later, on January 18, having missed an entire term while taking care of things back home. This time, however, Oxford felt different. All my cohorts had settled in, while I was a stranger. The culture shock could not have been greater. The city seemed alien, and the weather more so. The sun wouldn't come out for days, and the gloom got to me each and every day.

But there was no one to console me, no relatives to come home and show solidarity. My depression was intensely personal, and Oxford had no part to play in it. Not knowing how to cook added to my misery. The first few forays to the dining Hall of St. John's College, my alma mater, gave me a taste of food in Oxford.

Subsidised and bland, college food was, and still is, enough to sustain you for days, if taste wasn't much of a consideration. In winter, the temperature-controlled hall was a favourite refuge, and the piping hot cup of tea helped you start the day. But the moment you stepped out, the chill would take over.

When you are alone in such a situation, with no shoulder to cry on, you are forced to dig deep and find ways to survive. How long can you live with self-pity? I was a Rhodes scholar at Oxford, and many would give an arm and a leg to be in my place. I had to look at the Oxford experience as a challenge, and embrace it. Gradually, the cold became bearable. The bookstores were hugely alluring. The craft markets on Thursdays, where I could buy the occasional Neville Cardus for a pound, were treasure troves. Every trip to the Bodleian library was something to look forward to. The long walks during which I thought of my father allowed me to come to terms with his passing. At 24, I had no alternative but to take on the responsibility of sustaining the family. And now, at 46, I was back to square one. Two decades of work had been pushed to the fringes and my integrity questioned, all based on a pathetic victimhood card played to the hilt, sensationalism and social media vitriol. The only option left to me was to fight back.

I have walked on almost every street in Oxford. And usually done so alone. I know every bylane and every sandwich shop. Every ice-cream parlour too, since that was my indulgence in those days. Every Chinese takeaway. It is a city I consider home, where I lost and then again found myself, my bearings. A city that gave me the confidence to look forward and live after losing my father. It is a city that I had often gone back to whenever I needed to introspect. This time too, it was no different. I needed to get my confidence back and piece my life again together.

Before leaving for Oxford, however, something happened that really helped set things up. I left India on May 15, 2022. Just two days earlier, on May 13, Pullela Gopichand, one of my closest friends, visited Kolkata for a function. He was staying at the ITC Royal Bengal, and messaged me saying that he was coming to the city. Gopi and I go back to 2003-04, and have been extremely close friends ever since. While I wasn't really in the mood to meet anyone, I responded instinctively to Gopi's message, and asked him if he would like to meet for a few minutes. Within a minute, he responded saying that we must catch up. I still don't know if Gopi wanted to meet me to try and lift my spirits. I haven't asked him why he decided to reach out and fix the meeting. Knowing Gopi, that could well be the case, but it isn't something he would tell me or anyone else. Understated and calm, he is one of the best things to have happened to Indian sport.

The meeting was fixed for noon at the Royal Bengal's sky café, and Gopi was there on the dot. After exchanging pleasantries, he asked me what I thought of India's effort in the Thomas Cup. India was playing some exceptional badminton, and had beaten Malaysia 3-2 in a thrilling quarter-final the previous day to guarantee a first medal in 43 years. It was an occasion to celebrate.

'Don't you want to do an interview?' asked Gopi. I was taken aback. I hadn't really planned for one, and wasn't dressed to do a formal one either. But with the semi-final against Denmark to be played later that day, the timing couldn't have been better. As I said yes, I could see a smile on Gopi's face. He put his hand on my shoulder and said, 'We are all with you,' before looking away. For me, that was a huge moment. Just a week earlier, I had received a formal letter which stopped me from interviewing any contracted Indian cricketer, male or female, for two years. I had been punished for something I hadn't done—threaten a cricketer—and there was very little that I could do about it. Gopi's words came as both surprise and relief. They made me realise that individuals of substance still believed in me, despite the social media slander and character assassination.

Before we wrapped up, Gopi told me that he would happily put in a word with H.S. Prannoy, the star of the Thomas Cup triumph, if I was keen on talking to him. As I dropped him off at the airport later that day, I gave him an account of all that had happened. He did not say a word for almost the entire journey. But just as we were about to reach the terminal, he said something that I haven't forgotten. 'When you lost your father, you were forced to see the world differently and grow up,' he told me. 'You had no other alternative. This is yet one more occasion when you will grow up. Know the world better. And again, you don't have an alternative.'

That gave me the confidence to ask him something that was really important to me. I was planning to launch *Maverick Commissioner*, my new book that focussed on the cricket league, in Kolkata and Dubai in June, and was no longer in a position to call a cricketer to the events. Given that Gopi had worked on the Badminton League and observed the cricket league closely, would he come and release the book for me?

Gopi is an extremely busy man, and for him to come to Kolkata or Dubai at such short notice was near impossible. And yet, I asked him the question. I just had some inkling that he would agree. 'Let me do a video for the Kolkata launch and I will come to Dubai to do it for you,' he said. 'Fix it for June 26 in Dubai if you can, and let's record the video before I go into the airport.'

We both got out of the car just before reaching the departure terminal at Kolkata airport. Standing on the roadside, Gopi recorded a promotional video for *Maverick Commissioner*. It was a small one-minute video, but its significance for me went far beyond those 60 seconds. 'I did not win a medal at the 2000 Sydney Games,' he told me before heading inside to catch his flight. 'I should have and was ready. It isn't something I will ever forget. And trust me, it was one of the biggest disappointments of my life. But then, I did not give up. And may I say, I have been able to serve the sport and make a mark. In your case, this is a huge disappointment, yes, but it is also an opportunity to rediscover yourself and push the bar even higher.'

The world refers to Gopi as 'Sir'. He is the super coach. And in those few minutes, he had taught me a very important life lesson.

At a time when I couldn't do much in the cricket realm, the Thomas Cup win came as a huge opportunity. It was one of the greatest victories in the history of Indian badminton, and the *Times of India* had reported it as the sports lead, pushing the cricket news down to the lower half of the page. For me, it was an opportunity to reboot and chart out a route that I hadn't explored before.

India won the Thomas Cup the day I reached Oxford, and within moments of settling down in the hotel, I called Gopi to remind him to put in a word with Prannoy. He did so immediately, and the interview was fixed within the next couple of hours. I was back to doing what I had always done. Covering sport and telling stories. Prannoy's was a great tale, and to write on the Thomas Cup win was a journalist's delight. The interview went extremely well and was published in the *Economic Times* the following Sunday. The video, which I recorded while sitting in the gardens of the BW Linton Lodge Hotel in Summertown, was aired on RevSportz. There was abuse soon after the video went online, but with the subject being the Thomas Cup win and not cricket, it wasn't as vicious as before. By then, I had anyway gotten used to it. For me, the opportunity to work again and do what I loved was far more significant than some four-letter words on social media.

That was when the game actually changed. Soon after the ban, I was scared. I wasn't sure how I should react. I feared more waves of abuse and vitriol, and didn't know how to go about my work. I had never been the nervous sort, but the experiences of the previous two months had made me constantly look over my shoulder. I was very concerned about my mother, and felt that I had let the family down. How could I make them go through this hell? The moment I tried to get back to work, the cuss words would resume. I needed to overcome my anxiety and look ahead. Find validation in the process. The Thomas Cup win and Gopi helped me do so.

'Look, people don't matter,' Gopi told me when I called him

from Oxford. 'When you lost your father, did people come and take care of you or the family? When you worked on your books, did anyone else write them for you? When I train my players, do I train them for people? There is a world beyond people's likes and dislikes and abuse. And in that world, there is you, your work and your conscience. As long as you are clear about what you want to do and who you are, nothing else should matter to you. In fact, I would say that other sports will benefit from having you, now that you will cover more Olympic sport.'

That last sentence was accompanied by a chuckle. He had made me see the brighter side of things. I don't remember how many people watched the Prannoy interview. Or even if it got some good traction. Likes, retweets, quote tweets—nothing really mattered. All that did was reinstate my faith that I was doing my work again. The process and not the outcome. Not one troll mattered. Since then, I have happily blocked almost all those that came at me with abuse. And I'll continue to do so. Faceless cowards aren't worth engaging with, and what they say is about as significant as a fart in the ocean. Abuse is their only way of getting eyeballs, and of feeling significant. It was now time to plan the next two months, and do things that would help RevSportz grow. It had been my dream to set up and nurture a digital-first media company, which covered Olympic sport and cricket with equal passion. I had to start re-living that dream.

The picture

While in Oxford, my wife and I decided that we would go to Birmingham for a week, for that was where the Commonwealth

Games were to be held. And for India, the games had the potential be a watershed. There was a lot of buzz back home, and it was hoped that it would be the event where Indian athletes excelled. Not many of the established media houses send reporters to such events anymore, and we planned to bring a team of six so that we could cover most of the events in real time and with on-ground presence. The idea required meticulous planning and adequate funding, and a trip to Birmingham was essential. It is just an hour by train from Oxford, and we decided to make the most of our presence there. On the day of travel, Sharmistha clicked a picture of Aisha with me at the station, on the train to Birmingham. Me by the window and her next to me with her stuffed toys and drawing paraphernalia, all set for the journey. The usual father-daughter picture which you would have thought would be exempt from any kind of cricket-related abuse. But as I posted it, there were more than a few keyboard warriors lying in wait. One of the comments, which I remember even now, said, 'Now you don't have the money to travel by flight anymore, so you are now taking the train! Madar****'

Perhaps he had mistaken Leamington Spa, 20 minutes from Oxford by train, for Liluah, next to Howrah. But whether I had the money or not was no one else's business. This was just the two of us, father and daughter, enjoying a candid moment. That remark hit me like a freight train. I had had enough. The Cricketer needed to be made aware of the damage and devastation left behind in my life. This book had to be written.

5

Social Stigma

I turned 46 on March 8, 2022. Generally, friends and family start wishing you from midnight, and the greetings and banter continue for 24 hours or more on social media. I have always tried to respond individually to such messages. But beyond a point, individual responses aren't possible, and that's when you write a common message expressing gratitude for all the wishes. Even in the Covid years, 2020 and 2021, this was how things were. But 2022 had changed people around me.

While many still wished me on social media, some, steered clear of birthday greetings, in public at least. While writing this chapter, I checked all the messages that I have on my phone from that day. Three of them are reproduced here.

Message 1
'Dear _____, wish you a very happy birthday. Stay strong. You know I am always there to support you but it is best if you keep it low key this year.'

Message 2
'Happy birthday. Take care of the family and forget all that is going on. Don't be on social media and I am not wishing you on Facebook for the very same reason. A social media detox will do you good.'

Message 3
'This birthday will make you stronger. Wish you all the very best. I am deliberately not wishing you on twitter because it will just add to the situation.'

There are many more messages from friends on WhatsApp, who were scared to wish me on public platforms like Facebook and Twitter. Some felt it best to stay aloof for the time being, since I wasn't trending for the right reasons.

Interestingly enough, almost all of them wished me on social media in 2023 and 2024. Quite a few even posted pictures with me while wishing me the best 12 months ahead.

At the time, in March 2022, it hurt. Did people I had known for years actually believe even a part of what was being said about me? Could friendships be so shallow, and guided by the words of trolls?

A few friends who had vanished into the ether in February 2022 resurfaced around October that year, saying that their disappearing acts had been prompted by the need to give me breathing room. I thanked each one politely.

The fallout from the controversy extended to Sharmistha, my wife, as well. She was the one who usually dropped our daughter to school. Soon after the controversy became headline news, she could sense a few of the parents giving her the cold shoulder. Some even looked at her strangely. She wasn't affected, though. The fact that I was able to make it through the ordeal without losing my bearings was largely because of her unwavering support, which came to the fore again when we launched my next book, *Maverick Commissioner,* in Singapore in October 2022.

The Singapore release of the book had been planned for a while, and was being led by one of my partners at RevSportz. In hindsight, it was a hugely successful event, one that opened up a number of opportunities for RevSportz. However, the build-up to the event was complicated and a prime example of what I had to go through on account of the entire social media trial that I underwent.

We landed in Singapore, me, Sharmistha and Aisha, on the morning of October 1, with the book launch event scheduled for that afternoon. The plan was for us to meet with our partners for lunch at Tantra, a Bengali restaurant, and to then proceed to the venue together. Everything was fine up until that point. But upon reaching the restaurant, I was informed that one of the panellists at the launch had had to withdraw at the last minute, after being instructed to not associate with me. I was also told that one of the event's primary sponsors could back out at the eleventh hour, and that negotiations were ongoing. They too had been instructed by their India office that it wouldn't be good optics to support an event promoting the work of a social media pariah.

By then, none of this shocked me, but the only question I had was: 'Why now? Why on the day of the event?' I had not really wanted to do an event in Singapore. It was never my idea. But now, with everything finalised and invitations sent out, why these last-minute changes of heart?

I could see that my partner in Singapore, who had spent days organising the event, was visibly upset. On the one hand, he didn't want to see me uncomfortable or upset. On the other, the priority was to ensure that the sponsors did not walk away just hours before the event was to start. We reached a last-ditch compromise—the name of the sponsor would not be mentioned, and no one from the said organisation would come on stage at any point. They would go ahead and fund the event because it was something that they had committed to, and they did not want to leave us in a lurch. For them, proceeding with the event was like an act of generosity. A part of me had just wanted to cancel it. To proceed with a function where some of the hosts were reluctant participants was not something I was used to. Calling it off seemed the pragmatic option. But then, there were other sponsors involved, and all the invites had been sent. We just needed to grit our teeth and get through it. We reached the venue at 3:30 pm, 90 minutes before the event was to start. While the decision to go ahead was a collective one, there was a noticeable lack of excitement and none of the buzz you would normally associate with the build-up to a launch. Sharmistha had to remind me that I had seen worse, and that this was just another chapter in our fight for justice.

At Lounge 1883, where the event was being held, I could

sense some hostility from the audience. Almost everyone I was introduced to seemed reluctant to engage. There was little doubt that each one of them had read the things that had been written, in the press and on social media, and they seemed uncertain how to process it now that I was in their midst. So, when my partner invited me on stage to speak about the book, he was actually doing two things. He was giving me a platform to speak about my work and what it stood for. While not referring to the ban or the incident in any detail, there was enough for me to say. Secondly, it was an opportunity to talk briefly about RevSportz and the strides we, as a new company, had taken till then. I spoke for 45 minutes without a break and met the members of the audience eye to eye. I saw several nod intently. When I finally stopped, the first thing I noticed were the smiles. All of a sudden, the sponsors rushed to the stage and took ownership of the event. We clicked a hundred pictures thereafter, and all the apprehension disappeared. A number of people who were in the audience then are now friends and ardent supporters. Some have even invested in my company! I was able to narrate my experiences and my perspectives and worldview on sport, which possibly allowed people to take a more objective view of me. They might have been trying to make up their own minds as to whether I was the questionable character portrayed on social media, or a scholar of Indian cricket who had spent a quarter-century studying the game and wanting to make a difference.

Singapore was a small but significant victory, and it reinforced my belief that this book had to be written. People needed to be told my story so that they could separate fact from fiction. But the trip also brought home to me just how far the story had travelled, and the damage it had done to my reputation. In a previous era, a book launch in Singapore could be disconnected from something that had happened in India six months earlier. But in the social media age, such boundaries are porous and untenable. People and brands were still cagey about associating with me, and it was only after a long and personal interaction that they warmed up. While that was feasible in Singapore, with 150 people present in the audience, it was certainly not an option in the wider world where social media diktats held sway. Most folk form their opinions based on what they read and see splashed on social media platforms, and it is impossible to change perceptions overnight. The damage done was hardly the equivalent of a scratch on the paintwork. I just had to put my head down and get through it.

My Wikipedia profile was another easy target for online graffiti. The truth was that I had hardly ever used Wikipedia, since I didn't consider it reliable. However, while in Singapore, and just a day after the book launch, one of the members of the audience—now a friend and investor in RevSportz—sent me the link and asked why I was doing nothing about it. On reading it, my initial reaction was amusement. Trolls are easily identifiable most of the time, from their distant relationship with both coherent language and logic. Even by those low standards, this was a poor effort—a bunch of invectives in a language that I assumed was meant to be English. Instead of a profile, what the page had was a dismal attempt at vilification. Sharmistha was determined to not let it pass so easily. In fact, she painstakingly worked on the profile that evening, and also complained to the administrators about the abuse. For a few hours, the changes she made were on the page. But the very next day, the page had again been ambushed. I clearly had many admirers! This time round, I listed each factual error and filed a complaint. To be fair to Wikipedia, it was addressed, and while some of those in Singapore told me that I should also try and have the two lines that mentioned the ban removed, I was determined not to. The ban had become a badge of honour. And survival. It was a constant reminder that I couldn't shrink away from the injustice. Instead of being airbrushed out, it needed to be part of my profile so that I did not give up, and so that I could convince myself to get across to people the consequences of social media trials and kangaroo courts. If you go and check the Wikipedia page today, you will see those two lines about the ban. I hope those that read it will eventually go through this book as well. And then decide what to make of me.

There was a final meeting in Singapore that I wish to document, with a corporate who had significant investments in India and was extremely keen to be a part of the sports circuit. He had put money into a number of media start-ups, and I wished to meet him to discuss the possibility of his investing in RevSportz. He met me at the hotel, and as we settled down for a cup of tea, the conversation went thus:

X: So, when does this ban end?

Me: April 22, 2024.

X: Tell me something? Why did you get banned? Couldn't you

just have gone to The Cricketer, said sorry and closed the matter? Even if you were right, that would have been the prudent thing to do, isn't it?

Me: What?

X: Yes, because you have a company to run, and you need to be [working] in cricket to be able to make money. Why would you be headstrong and not compromise? Who gave you this advice? Why is morality so important? If I was in your position, I would have used my entire network to fix a meeting, and just got done with the issue. It would have been better for everyone. In fact, you should have put out a photograph shaking hands with The Cricketer, and then done an interview. It would have broken the Internet, and RevSportz would have gone places.

Me: Yes, perhaps you are right. We need to leave for the airport now, so maybe we could continue this over Zoom?

Was I naïve to not compromise and behave as I did? What this man said could well have been true. But then again, I was not him. He is who he is, and I am a struggling start-up entrepreneur! But however much I pondered over his advice, I couldn't get my head around the idea of putting the bottom line above the truth and self-respect. And may I say I am glad I am not him.

Aisha

My daughter is now 10, and like many other father-daughter relationships, it is a very special bond. We have our own little moments and games, which would make no sense to the world at large. We laugh over these things, and they make us happy.

Sitting and chatting with Aisha for hours is the best thing, and I constantly worry that she is growing up far too soon.

That's what brings me to the most distasteful accusation, which I found very hard to deal with. For being a father has, over these last years, brought out the best in me, be it compassion, nurture or just trying to be the best version of myself, for my family and especially my daughter—to be able to live up to her claim that I'm the best Boy in the world. To then read in the committee's report that The Cricketer actually alleged to have felt 'unsafe' and 'came to the airport in a different car rather than his own for the hearing', was for me the lowest ebb. If even someone had had considered me overbearing (and in that case he should have communicated that to me), it was like a violation of everything that I stood for to be told that I could harm or hurt. I ask The Cricketer to stand with me on any public platform, if he will, and enlighten us all and explain how exactly I made him feel quite so very threatened.

At the time of the incident, Aisha was not yet eight years old, and our first task was to insulate her from all that was going on. She wouldn't understand the seriousness of the situation, and it could have impacted her mental equilibrium. But this was the most difficult thing to do. How could I smile at her and do the things that we normally did when this fire was raging in the background? How could one lead two lives? Wouldn't she eventually understand that her father, normally a jovial outgoing person, was broken on the inside? That he sat alone in his study for hours on end without speaking to anyone, and only came down to the dining room to eat. As hard as I tried, I just couldn't shut out the noise. My little Aisha, sensitive as all children are, must have known something. She asked me dozens of times 'What happened?' It was only in Singapore months later that I decided to sit her down and tell her about the accusations against me. I have now told her everything, and while she may not have understood half of it, I took her into confidence. There was nothing to hide.

That was why I decided to take her to the book launch in Singapore. She sat in the audience and listened to me talk. She was in Class 3 then, and had started to read a lot of books. She could figure out what was going on, even if she found the event rather boring. We had made a deal beforehand. Lounge 1883 is located on top of a mall, and I had promised Aisha ice cream if she stayed quiet through the book launch. To my surprise, she did. In fact, it was only towards the very end of the session that she started gesticulating to me, asking how much time was still left. But she didn't say a word, and just saw and absorbed whatever she could. Soon after, when people started saying good things about me, I saw her smile. She enjoyed seeing the audience click pictures with her father, and realised that things had gone well.

As we had our ice cream afterwards, Aisha asked me a question with the refreshing bluntness that only children are usually capable of. 'Don't people know that my Boy (what she calls me) would never in his life harm anyone?' she said. 'You always give me whatever I want, and never scold me. Why would you harm someone else?'

No number of messages of support on social media would

have made the difference that that one remark did. For a father, it was the ultimate badge of honour. We are the best of friends and, hopefully, will always be. I have also read her sections of the book as and when we have had the time. Aisha knows how much this book means to me. Each time she came into my study to play and saw me writing, she would spontaneously say, 'Let me read *Secret Seven* for a while, and once you are done with your writing for the day, we can play.'

Imagine the same child seeing photos of ours on Twitter with the message underneath, '____'s daughter is really sweet. Only we feel sad that she was born to him. Pity the young kid.' She didn't only because she was eight then. Nobody spared a thought for her or her family. The person that unleashed this on me knew full well that like him I too have a family, I too have a child.

That message lamenting Aisha's misfortune as my daughter, was one of thousands, that too phrased in a manner that was not sickening and abusive, like many of the rest. And all of this while The Cricketer continued to tell the media that he had to rake up the issue again and again, in successive media interviews, because there was no public apology forthcoming from me. To the committee, he said that he had heard rumours that his contract with his cricket league franchise would be terminated. On my account? How so? Since when did journalists start to decide the composition of these teams? If I had that kind of influence or power in the cricket world, would I have been banned for two years? It is a question I now dare him to answer after my two years of enduring hell.

Each time The Cricketer spoke, the jibes and insults would

spike again. Was it deliberate? While I don't have any evidence, the timing of some of his statements was particularly interesting.

For the first week, he was on an interview-giving spree. Most of these chats are still available on social media, and the central message in each is the same. While saying that he did not want to harm me, he explained that he had no option but to come forward and protect future generations of cricketers. In the absence of an apology from me, what else could he do?

Brutus is an honourable man.

The second round of speaking out happened just days before a conclave done by RevSportz on March 21, 2022, focussing on one of the teams of the cricket league. I have already described this elsewhere in the book. Suffice to say that had The Cricketer's interview of that day been aired, headlined as it was and pitched as 'being the first time he was giving out the full story', the conclave would have been destroyed. The trolls would have been rejuvenated, and I would have been trending again.

The third round of The Cricketer's interviews, apparently coincidentally, were done just a couple or so days after the launch of my book *Maverick Commissioner* in Kolkata on June 16. I was banned on April 23, and that year's cricket league ended on May 28. Frankly, the issue was dead by then, and I had been put away. So why rake it up again? To what effect? And that too just a few days after the stupendous success of the launch of my book.

Serendipity? I don't think so.

And then once again, another round of articles were published. Evidently some of the journalists of leading national dailies had not had enough of the matter or of The Cricketer's allegations, now rehashed several times. Here is a sample of what was published in a leading daily on June 22, 2022, just five days after the *Maverick Commissioner* event in Kolkata. By then, the book was already on the bestseller list.

'If the person doesn't even have regret, how can you stay silent?': ____ makes big revelation on journalist controversy ____ opened up on the controversy, that resulted in the journalist being banned for two years. On February 19 of this year, ____ on his official Twitter profile, had called out journalist ____ for using intimidatory language on messaging application 'WhatsApp'. ____ had shared screenshots of his conversation with ____ after the player did not revert to his request for an interview.

After over four months since the incident, ____ opened up on the controversy, revealing that the journalist has 'done such things before' as well.

'My purpose was to show that a journalist can go to these lengths to get an interview. I got to know later that he has done such things before as well, that is why ____ stepped in and punished him. I didn't speak initially because I'm under contract with ____'

____ further added that ____ didn't show any regret for his actions, which prompted the player to go public with the screenshots.

'I also didn't feel like speaking about it in the first place, because at the end of the day, everyone has their own careers. But if the other person doesn't even have any regret, how long can you stay silent?'

My silence on the issue (I had not spoken to a single media outlet after the ban, and did not on the issue through the two years of the ban) was evidently an admission of guilt, and evidence of my lack of remorse. But wait, remorse for what?

If I have any sorrow, it is for my family, for what they were made to go through on account of my social media trial. Also, I do regret something, and very much so. For not hitting back at the allegations of the matter and putting out my side that *very first night* of The Cricketer's tweets. For staying silent, for trying to de-escalate the matter which I thought then was a simple misunderstanding, and for trying to reach out to friends in the cricket world hoping it was the best thing under those circumstances. Let me advise as one who has suffered the worst. If you are being targeted, do not lie low. No matter what anybody tells you, defence is not the best strategy. I should never have had to write this book. I should have put out my earlier chats with The Cricketer on social media, like he did. This book should have been written that very first night, in a form that was meant for the very same social media platform. It could have exposed some things there and then. That is one regret I do have.

The victim cult, a popular calling card across walks of life, ended up doing irreparable damage to my family and career, and also my company and team members who suffered through these two years along with me.

The negativity was evident even a year and a half after the incident when Ridhima Pathak, anchor and sports presenter who had worked with me in the past, invited me to be on a show for her YouTube Channel. Ridhima has evolved as a sports presenter, and it is impressive to see her doing multi-sport content, a rarity among anchors, and I had no hesitation in agreeing to do the show.

We had fixed a 9 pm slot for the recording, but I did not

know that Ridhima had put out a poster on X (formerly Twitter) asking for questions from anyone interested. She was keen to speak to me about football, cricket and the Asian Games, to try and understand where we stood at the time. The poster evoked a mixed response. While some fans responded asking questions about the Indian football team's participation at the Asian Games, a story I was covering hands-on at the time, others asked about the impact of franchise leagues on the future of international cricket. But about 10 to 15 per cent of the responses, so many months after the ban, and which are still on X went in the below mould:

'Iss ch*tiya ko kahan se laya?'

'Dislike Button.'

'Ask him why did he snoop on _____?'

Another just said, 'No Please.'

None of these people has ever spoken to me. They don't even remotely know me. And yet, they were happy to call me names on a public platform. While that is how social media functions, it was interesting that the matter was alive in public memory even after a year and half—very much against the social media trend of skipping from issue to issue with the attention span of gnats.

If ever I needed proof for why this book was needed, it was there in front of me. In my case, there was never any question of forgive and forget. The issue hasn't been forgotten, and for my part, I am clear—I am not ready to forgive.

I have been asked my reasons for writing this book by those in the know, and remember discussing it with my publishers. In fact, a close friend who is also a very well-known journalist, said to me: 'Your company is now recognised across the country. For a brand that is two years old, that is a very special achievement. You did some fantastic cricket interviews during the last World Cup on Indian soil without breaking a single sanction. Olympic sport is your forte. I can't count the number of interviews you have done across Olympic sports in two years. Most importantly, 2024 is an Olympic year and you will surely excel at the Olympics and Paralympics. Why do you want to attract negativity to the platform when things are going so well for you? The ban is over in April 2022. Why don't you just move on? Everyone knows you are good, and you will get your network back in cricket as well.'

The gentleman in question is a well-wisher, and it was not a snide comment. What he said made a lot of sense. This book is a risk, and a big risk that I decided to take. The question was simple—was it worth taking? Could it harm RevSportz, and was I prepared to deal with another period of turmoil?

For me, the answer is very clear. Yes, I am prepared for the risks. Unlike that night of the first tweets by The Cricketer which left me flummoxed, this time I have an understanding of what was done to me and why. I have never had more clarity about anything in my life. This has nothing to do with business or RevSportz or material gain. Rather, it is about who I am. My identity. My family, and our humiliation of the last two years. So, yes, it is a risk worth taking, to put my word out there. When I did well during my MA examinations as a student of Presidency College, Kolkata, getting record marks in history, many felt that I should go ahead and pursue a PhD in something conventional. The trends of the time were agrarian history or industrial or women's history. Studies of popular culture were relatively rare and Indian sports scholarship non-existent. When I suggested to my professors that I would like to work on the history of cricket in India, they were shocked. Some even said I was jeopardising what could be a fantastic career. My life was at a crossroads. To be honest, I had no money then, my father had died very suddenly and the family was in debt. But I decided to pursue my dream nonetheless. For my PhD at the University of Oxford, I worked on the history of Indian Cricket (possibly the only one in the subject at that institution), and it was in the field of that very same sport that I gained my first on-field and professional experience as a journalist. Cricket has been at the centre of my heart, and unlike when I was 24, I now have friends and a strong family to stand by me. People who know what I stand for. I have RevSportz, and colleagues who know the truth for what it is. If I could put my career on the line at 24, when I started to do my thesis on Indian cricket, why would I not take a risk now and publish this book? If nothing else, for my love of the very same sport and what it stands for—*fair play, and then fair play, and once again, fair play*. Why fear a backlash and step back? When I have a body of work spanning more than two decades to back me up.

While growing up, I was taught that the truth eventually comes out, no matter how long it takes. No matter how entitled somebody maybe, and no matter how loud the noise around them, life has strange ways of catching up, with everybody. Time could turn a narrative on its head. If no one ever raised their voices against the entitled, then would there have been revolts from below or a country's struggle for independence? Humanity has always found its voice when confronted with injustice, freedom in the arms of duress. For that freedom, risk is a small price to pay. If speaking out harms me, or RevSportz (and possibly it will), so be it.

6

Media Matters

It had been four days since The Cricketer had first tweeted, and we had a team meeting at my house to decide on future strategy. Several colleagues felt that I should not go on air or do a show for two weeks because that would only add to the abuse. The idea was to suspend the programme flow, and reassess at the beginning of March. The meeting was to work out that plan. We had a small team then and almost all of us were together by 2:30 pm, when Debasis Sen walked in looking grim and anxious. '_____ is constantly calling me to go on his show, and tell him something about you,' he blurted out. 'I don't want to take any more calls.'

The said journalist had replaced me at my previous media organisation after I left the organisation in October 2021. My nine years with the group had been some of my most enjoyable in the media. For that entire time, I had known the said journalist reasonably well. While we weren't best friends, I always considered him a decent reporter. So, I was more than just a little taken aback when Debasis said this to me in front of the entire team. Just as I was about to respond, his phone rang again. And it was the same person.

I gestured to him to put the phone on speaker mode, which Debasis immediately did. While the conversation wasn't recorded, there were at least six people who could testify as to what they heard for the next few minutes. The said journalist was pushing (an evidently discomforted) Debasis hard to come on his show, saying things like 'Just tell me what ____ is thinking of doing. And it's him right, who has sent the messages? Just confirm that on my show. That's all we need from you. He deserves to be named, for it will help stop such incidents in future.'

Pressuring?? For an exclusive? Bullying?

I could not believe what I was hearing. My first thought was to call his senior, who I still consider a friend, and tell him what I had just heard. The said individual was in charge of the entire sports coverage for the very same group after I left, and he needed to know what the said journalist was up to. But then, could this have happened without his knowledge? Could the journalist in question call someone at RevSportz, and try to prevail on him to speak against his own colleague and senior, without the journalist's own senior being in the loop? I still don't have an answer for this, but at that moment, I decided not to make the call. And while our paths have crossed multiple times since, I haven't broached the subject with anybody.

As for the journalist that tried to pressure Debasis into speaking against me, he could at least have called me. Or even texted to ask for my side of the story, whether he then believed it or not. What we are taught as journalists, something reinforced from the day you join an organisation as a trainee, is that there are two sides to every tale. Basic journalistic ethics require you to piece together all the details before arriving at a conclusion. The said journalist had chosen his side without bothering to even ask my side of the story. He had swallowed the popular narrative, and identified the fall guy, because that was the easiest and the 'done' thing at the time. Doing anything different would need the courage to stand up to the troll army, and that takes some doing. This journalist, very conveniently, was now one of the crusaders who wanted to teach me a lesson. And he wanted to do it using one of my own confidants.

Mama, as Debasis is fondly called by one and all, was visibly shaken. 'How can he ask me to do this?' he said, looking crestfallen. 'How can someone who has known you for years not even check with you what happened?' But then, this behaviour was no aberration. The YouTube channel for which this journalist had sought Debasis' interview, and which I had helped build, did the most shows on the issue and never bothered to call me even once. And its sister sports platform, which I had contributed to a lot during the 2019 World Cup, ranked a close second. It was a concerted campaign.

Two former colleagues at the same group called me. The first was a senior journalist who is also the son of a former cricketer, who said he was concerned and understood what I was going through. He said that he was with me in spirit, but there was little he could do. He alluded to a lot of things being talked about in the newsroom, but said that he had distanced himself from the matter. Since then, he and I have kept in touch.

The second person to reach out was the Editor of the group's flagship Hindi channel. The said individual is one of the best-mannered television professionals I know, always polite and courteous. We shared the most cordial bond during my time at my former organisation, and he called to say that I should take care of myself and the family, and that this too would pass. He asked if I needed any help. I thought of the above-mentioned journalist's attempts to drag my name through the muck and through pressuring my own colleague at RevSportz, but decided against mentioning it. The said individual had called me as a friend, and not as the channel's Editor.

Since then, I have met the journalist that called Debasis, on multiple occasions. He even walked up to me to say hello during the World Test Championship (WTC) final in London in June 2023. I did not say a word on the subject. In fact, I have nothing further to say to this individual. May I also say here, that persons like him stand in a sharp contrast to somebody like Debasis, whose integrity was, and stays, unshakeable—he stands not for me, but for what he believes is the truth. For what he saw play out in front of his own eyes, and nothing could ever make him change his version. He was with me that evening of the cricket league's auction when the call was made to The Cricketer, who had then agreed to do the interview with me. Debasis had followed up on my behalf after the zoom link was sent for the interview.

The journalist that tried to pressure Debasis was someone I had known reasonably well for several years, but we were never friends as such. But there were others who I had considered like brothers. S____ Sports Editor at a Bengali daily, and I had been buddies for more than a decade. I had written blurbs for his books, and even launched and reviewed some of his novels. We had planned special projects together and, at a time when things weren't going well for him, he would regularly come to my house to unwind. The least I expected of him was that he would call to ask for my side of the story before going on to write whatever he wanted to.

At this point, I need to make one thing very clear. I have nothing to say against anyone that wrote against me or said things on television. It was not a situation created by them but their response to that situation. If they felt I was in the wrong, they were entitled to do so. But in this case, I had known S____ for decades. Before writing op-eds belittling me and adding to the abuse on social media, the least he could have done was talk to me and get my side of the story, if even what he wrote thereafter was negative. My door was not shut in his face. My phone was never switched off. He could have been objective rather than one-sided. Rational rather than sensationalist. He even went to the extent of ridiculing my name, several times in the op-ed, which was in extreme poor taste. For almost three weeks, this newspaper carried copies almost daily on the issue. Not once was I asked my version of events. This was all the more surprising because I used to write a column for them at the time. While I understood the decision to suspend that, I considered it deeply unfair that I was given no chance to defend myself.

I met the Editor of the very same newspaper after three months, and shared with him every little detail of what had transpired. He is someone I have known more than 20 years, and to be fair to him, he was unaware of these articles that had appeared in the sports pages. After hearing my side, he asked how he could possibly help, and since then, the paper in question has reviewed two of my books, and we have been in touch often. As for S_____, he came up to me and tried to start a conversation at the Tollygunge Club, when I hosted a function on April 21, 2023, on the occasion of a book launch. He said I was doing some excellent work. And naturally! By then RevSportz was on an upward curve!

The timing of the friendly approach was instructive. That morning, *Sangbad Pratidin* had carried an almost-full-page report of my visit to Sachin's house for his birthday, where we formally launched *Sachin@50*. And despite India's present-day cricketers and stadia being out of reach because of my ban, India's greatest Olympians—Neeraj Chopra, Abhinav Bindra and PV Sindhu, to name just three—were always happy to share their thoughts. RevSportz had done some quality work, including India's biggest sports conclave in March 2023, and with *Sachin@50* coming close on the heels of that, I was no longer just a punching bag. It was time to befriend me again!

Another episode stands out. On the evening of June 16, *Maverick Commissioner*, my book on Lalit Modi and the cricket league, was launched at the ITC Sonar in Kolkata. To my pleasant surprise, a number of senior editors and media figures turned up. One of them came up to me said, 'You must be feeling vindicated. The whole of Kolkata has turned up for you. Clearly, this is proof the city is with you and not against you.' I had known him for years, and written for his pages for close to a decade. That was what compelled me to ask then, why he had allowed the publication of a series of articles against me, without bothering to check what I had to say on the subject. We had been friends for years, so I asked him without bothering to sugar-coat the question. 'It's time you forget it and moved on,' was his response. 'We will set things right.'

Simple words, but devoid of meaning. Dismissive almost. I was being asked to forget abuse, which had traumatised my 73-year-old mother, a diabetic, whose blood-sugar levels had shot through the roof after reading all that had been written about her son. I was being told to overlook the slurs directed at my wife on social media. And last, but by no means the least, I was being asked to gloss over the fact that my eight-year-old daughter had been branded, on social media, as the child of a bully.

How could I forget that I had lost work and contracts, and been targeted to such an extent that I almost lost my livelihood? And that on the night of May 5, 2022 tried to do something to myself? I have no qualms in admitting that I had contemplated doing something drastic to myself on more than one occasion, but better sense prevailed. It was impossible for me to forget any of that. And I never will. But then, what could I say to him?

The franchise fiasco

While I was being trolled and disparaged, I received strong support from unexpected quarters—the senior management of one of the teams of the cricket league who had known me personally and professionally, and to which The Cricketer was contracted. Within a week of the incident, I got a call from a senior functionary, who asked me my side of the story. And on hearing it, he promised me that the franchise wouldn't allow The Cricketer to use their platform to air any personal issues. I was also told that they had had a chat with The Cricketer the moment he had joined the camp, and it was agreed that this issue would not become a talking point so far as the social media platforms of the franchise were concerned. It was a personal matter between him and a journalist, and nothing to do with the franchise.

I was further surprised when they reached out and asked if I wanted to interact with their squad. After all, The Cricketer was part of it, and I hadn't expected to be told that I could interview some of their key personnel for my show. On March 23, we even did a conclave, featuring ten of their key players for RevSportz. The CEO of the franchise, and the head of cricket were also part of it, and it was the most comprehensive coverage on the franchise's preparation ahead of their first season in the cricket league.

I should have known though that it wouldn't all be smooth sailing. There was unnecessary drama which needs to be documented for the readers' benefit. Ahead of their first year in the league, the franchise had hired a lady as their digital media head. Before joining them, the very same lady had worked on the cricket league's auction for RevSportz. The idea was to have her as our primary anchor throughout the tournament, a plan that had to be canned once she got the franchise job. She had hosted all our auction shows, and also done some interviews in the lead-up to it. She was also part of the RevSportz panel for the Women's World Cup, which was being played in New Zealand at the time. It was natural that she knew my side of things, as I had spoken to her on multiple occasions as things unravelled.

After this lady joined the franchise, I assumed that she had been the one behind arranging all the interviews for my show. I couldn't have been more wrong. At around 9 pm on the evening on March 21, I got a call from my friend Arani, who is a fellow journalist. I had finished dinner and was reading when Arani, a rather calm and relaxed person, called in a state of anxious excitement. 'Have you seen what was put out?' he asked. I hadn't noticed anything untoward, and when I told him as much, he seemed relieved. 'I am glad you did not,' he said, before getting Kushan into a conference call. 'The franchise's Twitter handle put out a 50-second clip from an interview with The Cricketer, which said he would soon reveal the real story behind what happened,' said Kushan. 'There was no reason for this to happen now, and we called the senior management to ask what was going on.' Within minutes of their call, the clip had been deleted across all their social-media platforms. At best, it had been online for about 30 minutes.

Coming just two days before our conclave, the timing of the clip was off. Was it a deliberate attempt to rake up the issue that had settled a wee bit? My silence had been perceived as weakness and an admission of guilt. With The Cricketer speaking on the issue yet again, the backlash would start again, the abuse on social media that had targeted me and completely unsettled my family life. Could it really be that I would be allowed no peace? I was angry and frustrated, and I messaged one of the key people in the franchise set-up to ask what was going on. Within minutes, I had an answer. I was told that what had happened was wrong and those responsible had already been pulled up and reprimanded. The franchise did not believe in taking sides, and wouldn't allow their platforms to be used to push any kind of agenda. I was assured of that, and told to go ahead with the conclave plan. I did eventually see the clip, which was sent to me by someone within the franchise management.

So, did the lady in question, who had also worked for RevSportz, have a role to play in putting out the clip? I recall asking the franchise top brass, for she did oversee their digital-media platforms. I find it unfathomable that she would have allowed something like that to happen on her watch, despite knowing my account. Unlike the many others who had blindly pronounced me guilty, she actually knew my side of the story. Technically, she was still working for RevSportz, with the Women's World Cup on, but I did not bother to ask her and risk souring things further. I still don't know for certain what part she played, but as content lead, it was her domain.

What I do know is that the franchise let her go at the end of the season, and The Cricketer's interview never saw the light of day. My relationship with the senior management continues to be excellent, and each one of them knows my truth. We have discussed the matter in some detail and their stance remains the same—it was something that happened between The Cricketer and I, and they had no interest in picking a side. I respect that. For the record, one of the last interviews I did after the controversy erupted and before the Apex Body imposed sanctions was with a cricketer owned by the same franchise. He had enjoyed two fantastic seasons with the franchise, who facilitated what was a very good interaction. Being allowed to interview some of their leading stars was vindication in itself. It told me that they were not interested in sitting in judgment without knowing all the details. Despite the controversy and its aftermath, I probably interviewed more players from this particular franchise than any other journalist in 2022. I would like to believe that they wouldn't have allowed that to happen if they thought me a bully. I wouldn't even say that some of my fellow media professionals and former colleagues actually believed it (had none of them ever sought exclusives?!), even though they tried to fan the flames for as long as they could. However, it was a chance to decimate a tough competitor, and few gave that chance a miss.

'You fetch social-media likes'

It was October 2022, and I was on my way to Australia for the T20 World Cup. I was checking in at Kolkata Airport when I got a call from Subhayan Chakraborty, one of my colleagues. He asked if I was amenable to two young and aspiring social media influencers working with him on a show on domestic cricket. I had always wanted to promote domestic cricket on the RevSportz platform. But when he mentioned their names to me, a switch was flicked in my head. These two gentlemen, whom I have subsequently come to know reasonably well, had both posted multiple tweets against me during the controversy. How was it that they wanted to work on a platform I had founded? I did not tell Subhayan any of this, of course, and just asked him to send me their numbers so that I could have a word. I intended to ask them why they had written what they had. Were they asked to do so by somebody? Why else would two young cricket enthusiasts, who did not even remotely know me, jump on the bandwagon and take a public stand against me without having a clue as to what had really happened?

Within moments, Subhayan had sent me the numbers. I called them from the lounge of the International Airport. Again, Debasis was with me, as we were traveling together on the Singapore Airlines flight. The conversations were startling. Both chats exposed the deep malaise that has now got social media in a vice-like grip. When I introduced myself, one of them seemed a little taken aback. That was before he told me that it would be great if we could work together. I said I had no problem with anyone doing quality work on the RevSportz platform, but I needed to know who, or what, had prompted him to target me in April 2022.

'If I have to be honest and tell you the truth, it was the done thing then,' he replied, a little sheepishly. 'A tweet against you would fetch 500 likes, and add to my subscriber base.' I couldn't believe what I was hearing. He and his friend had indiscriminately attacked a complete stranger, in exchange for some social media likes and an increased subscriber base. Not sparing a thought about the person's family or their mental health. At the same time, I was pleased that this young man spoke the truth. It showed courage of a kind to at least explain why he had done what he did. Each of these men are in their twenties, young and impressionable minds whose lives are controlled by the number of likes or followers on Twitter and Instagram. A few hundred likes give them some kind of high, almost like a drug, and a few thousand subscribers means that you have arrived. The addition of another thousand subscribers usually means a celebratory card thanking the 'Twitter family' and the like. They haven't seen enough of the world yet to realise just how fleeting these things are. That, in the final analysis, none of this really matters. What does is hard work, and how willing you are to go the extra mile.

The second response was even more revealing. 'When it is between you and a cricketer, it is natural which side one should be on,' the second gent told me. 'However popular you are or whatever work you may have done as a journalist, public sentiment will always be with the cricketer. So it was natural that I would tweet in his favour. If I tweeted supporting you, I would have been trolled brutally.' Again, the honest confession brought a wry smile to my face. I was face-to-face with ground realities that I was well aware of, but had never really had to confront. This is what a social media witch-hunt is all about. The side that makes the most noise, or amplifies it cleverly, always wins. A pre-existing position of social acceptance, the status of being a star in the public imagination and having that privilege (and hence a certain position of power), unlike a journalist, also becomes a clincher. Reason and logic don't often stand a chance.

When you have a deluge of articles being written on an issue, all pointing fingers at one individual, and there are hundreds of thousands of social-media posts pronouncing that person guilty, perhaps a committee is also driven by this wave of public opinion? A body representing Indian cricketers had also written to the Apex Body asking it to investigate the matter, based on the social media outrage. I was the victim of a media trial based on testimony from someone of stature, who used his position as a well-known entity with a much greater social media following than myself, to garner public sympathy on social media. In the days after he was dropped from the test squad, social media was used to project him as the plucky underdog (a stance that sells like no other in the popular imagination) rather than a person of eminence and entitlement. Kangaroo courts have existed since the beginning of time, but social media has amplified their power manifold.

After it imposed sanctions on me, the Apex Body continued granting accreditations to other journalists and reporters from RevSportz. Possibly they understood that livelihoods were at stake, and that RevSportz wasn't just me. I founded the company, but we now employ more than 30 professionals. RevSportz has been accredited for all ICC events, and there has never been any obstruction in the workflow. And when I met some of the senior Apex Body functionaries at The Oval during the WTC final, there was no unpleasantness or unease. I did not utter a word about the ban, because I had chosen to live through it and serve the ban before I opened up. Not because I respected the sentence against me, but because I was mindful of it. Now that the ban is behind me, it is imperative that I reveal the sequence of events.

Selling misery and humiliation

The day before the launch of *Maverick Commissioner*, my book which is now being made into a movie by Vibri Motion Pictures, the PR agency that was working on the invites called me at 3 pm. 'No media wants to come to the event,' they told me. 'We don't know what to do. The moment we say it is your book, everyone is backing out. The very same people were keen on attending every event you did in the past.'

I was not surprised. I had been side-lined and 'disgraced', and it was natural that the media would choose to stay away. But the PR agency's representative offered a caveat. 'However, if we tell them who are the people on the panel, they will come,' they said.

'I will not give out a single detail,' I replied. 'Whoever wishes to come will come, and whoever wishes to stay away, that's fine by me. I run a media company, and we will cover the event ourselves.' I disconnected the call.

Within minutes, they had called me back. 'Will you speak on the ban?' they asked. 'If you do, everyone will come.'

Maverick Commissioner had nothing to do with my ban. It was a book I had worked on for years. It is the backstory of the cricket league, and how Lalit Modi helped create the league but could not stay in control of it. It is a gripping tale, and by agreeing to speak on the completely unrelated ban, I would have done serious injustice to four years of effort. I refused, and had not even a second thought about doing so.

The media nonetheless turned up for the launch, and the coverage we got was phenomenal. But that's a different story, and not really relevant to this one.

Within an hour of my interaction with the PR agency, I got a call from a fellow journalist, who had been running a digital sports platform for the past couple of years. He and I had been colleagues at my previous media organisation, and he had since left to work on his own projects. I had been in touch with him, and had invited him to cover the launch just as I had everyone else in the media. He had responded favourably, and suggested that we touch base closer to the event. He had a background in cinema, and was an entertainment anchor to begin with. His platform had reasonable viewership, and given that the book was being made into a film, he seemed a perfect fit to cover the launch.

'I can come, but then it is essential that I ask you about what really happened with The Cricketer story,' he told me. 'How can I not address the elephant in the room? All my viewers will want to know, and after the first two questions, we can talk about the book at length.'

Anything I said on the ban would sell. That was the real headline, not the book that he was being invited to cover. Having been in the media business for nearly 25 years, I had the sense to understand what he was indicating. He would cover the event provided I spoke to him, exclusively, about the ban. Having decided that I wouldn't say a word on the subject, I told him as much. I said that he was welcome to ask whatever he wanted to, but all I would say in response was that this was not the forum to discuss the matter. I would speak about it at a later date. I was very clear about that.

My understanding was that he would back off after hearing me and not bother coming for the launch. But he did turn up, and we did do the interview. He asked me exactly what he had suggested, and I answered exactly as I had told him I would. Not a word more. I said nothing to him about The Cricketer. Absolutely nothing. And yet, he went and headlined his story with the controversy, saying that this was the first time I was speaking on the issue. He even put out a trailer where I could be seen saying that this wasn't the occasion to speak (on the issue of The Cricketer and me). It ended by asking people to watch the full interview.

This is a much-used tactic. Viewers would come to find out what had really happened with The Cricketer and me, and end up watching the interview on his channel. The video is still there on his YouTube channel at the time of this book going to press, and with over 127,000 views. Most of the comments are abuse directed at him, saying that he was critical of me during the controversy and had done an about turn, and questioning why he was posing for pictures with me at the book launch. Some even went on to ask where it was that I had spoken about the issue, and why he had misled his viewers. They were right. I hadn't addressed either The Cricketer or the ban, and the headline was poles apart from the actual content. But for this fellow journalist of mine, it was important to be sensationalist—to get more people to his platform. That's how he spun the story.

And it wasn't just him. This seems to be the norm nowadays, and I wasn't at all surprised that he followed the click-bait template. Only, in his case, it was doubly strange because he had posted a series of tweets against me in April—which I saw only after the book launch—and there he was in June, posing with my book. I hadn't seen his earlier tweets because after a point I had shut myself off from social media while the controversy raged. It was better to go into a cocoon and keep my head above water.

The journalist in question isn't the issue here. He is just representative of a widespread problem. Was he actually against me? No, he wasn't. At least, I don't think so. Had that been the case, he wouldn't have come to the launch and extended a hand of support. Just like the two young social media influencers, he too tried to pluck as many low-hanging social media fruits as he could. A provocative tweet or two would fetch him several hundred likes and a couple of hundred new followers. You need such numbers to attract potential sponsors, and be paid as an influencer. So what if someone else was harmed in the process? In the rat race, no one stops to turn the moral compass on themselves. All that is expected is that you break stories or package them in a manner that sells. As I saw him being trolled with screenshots of his earlier tweets, someone I know got right to the heart of the matter. 'He will yet again add subscribers, and get his videos seen,' they said. 'So don't worry about it.'

Ethics? Not everyone's cup of Darjeeling.

7

Ashwin and the Flight Back to India

Call it coincidence, or what you will. On my flight back after the deferred England-India Test match at Edgbaston in July 2022, I was pleasantly surprised to find Ravi Ashwin, one of my favourite players and someone I know really well, in the seat immediately in front of me. It had been Mayank Agarwal on the way to Birmingham. Now, it was Ashwin. The cricket Gods, it seemed, were intent on testing me.

I had known Ashwin for years, and he is someone with a mind of his own—a rebel in his own sort of way. He is not just one of the best bowlers India and the world has seen, but also extremely feisty and strong-willed. Anyone who watched him bat in extreme pain at the Sydney Cricket Ground in January 2021 would know what I am referring to. He speaks his mind, and isn't afraid to be politically incorrect. In fact, one of the best interviews I had done for RevSportz was with Ashwin, where he opened up on issues of mental health, how he planned his game and what cricket meant to him. With Ashwin, you could always speak your mind without fear of being judged.

Soon after we bumped into each other on the flight, he asked how things were with me. 'I did not want to call you then, for it did not feel or seem right,' he told me. 'At times, it is best to just let things be and not ask. That's the best way with friends. I did not need to call you to tell you I am your friend. We both know it. I know you have the ability to get things right and, over time, you will. You love the sport, and your work speaks. It will be alright.'

Simple words that made a lot of sense. What could he have said to me at the time? A call would only have made things awkward. Ashwin wasn't a journalist and, for him, I wasn't a story. I was somebody who was going through a rough time. He wasn't judging me. Nor was he judging The Cricketer. He did not know what really happened, nor was he keen on gossip. He thought it best to give me some space. I appreciated what he said, and neither of us spoke more about the issue. Instead, we had a chat about the Tamil Nadu Premier League (TNPL), and how keen he was to get back to playing T20 cricket with the World T20 in Australia.

After we landed, I was waiting for Trisha Ghosal to join me, for we had a connecting flight to Kolkata. Ashwin was on a flight to Chennai, and needed to rush. I was surprised to see him waiting for me at the top of the escalator. He said he had something to say before we parted ways. 'This will test you, but if you are true to yourself, you will come through it well,' he said, before wishing me luck.

Certain relationships are not defined by self-interest. My association with Ashwin is one such.

'These kinds of journalists are tumours that are slowly turning into cancers. They will take away the game's respect in front of the public.'—Abhishek Kumar Singh, April 27, 2022.

Really?

Here are the salient points from the hatchet-job masquerading as an article:

'For an individual like ____ even respect for cricketers like ____ does not appear in the dictionary…'

'It may be true that ____ had an influence in ____ getting dropped from the team as there was a 6-day gap between ____ messages and ____ getting snubbed from the team. ____ role is a realistic possibility…'

This journalist, if I can call him that, had written a fairly long piece on the matter four days after the Apex Body had announced the sanctions against me. Such poison-pen copies were the flavour of the season, and even today, his rant is one of the most-read pieces on that platform. Frankly none of the other pieces have any readers!

Did he bother to call me and check if there was a version of events different from that in the social media domain? No. You would expect that to be the least a journalist did before referring to someone by name as a tumour or cancer in print.

Like thousands of others, he didn't have a clue to what had

The multiple tweets and exchanges with the cricketer, which clearly establish the proximity. The question is would these tweets be done for a bully or for one who used to threaten? May be not.

28/11/19

Excited about the #Inspiration series on " ". Looking forward to watch this one. @BoriaMajumdar #Inspiration

Boria Majumdar 28/11/19

get well soon and look forward to your feedback. Thank you.

28/11/19

Thank u Boria da. Your show will be a blockbuster. My best wishes as always.

Thank You for having me @BoriaMajumdar ! Loved the chat session with you, & 👍👍

Boria Majumdar 04 Nov 20

Thanks for coming on the show and what a superb chat we had. thanks both for making it so good. Anyone who missed please watch and let ys know......

25 Nov 20

Thank You so much! @BoriaMajumdar

Boria Majumdar 24 Nov 20

Hey wish you a very happy and safe bday and ofc Subho ashtami. Bhalo theko. Need you in Australia at your best.

21/02/22

He

One of several thousand tweets. By the way dogs are best friends. Far more loyal and committed than trolls who will never understand such relationships.

The Gopi interview that made for a restart.

Javed Saab said he was doing the Sourav 50th birthday poem for me. In July 2022, it meant the world coming from him. This was in London when he recited the poem for us.

CWG 2022 in Birmingham

Athletes made the games for Revsportz and we were noticed nationally. I did not have accreditation but it did not stop India's best from speaking to me.

Odisha

New opportunities opened up and to be able to document the Odisha story was one such. My sincere gratitude to Hon. CM Shri Naveen Patnaik and it was a pleasure to work with my co-author Shri Vineel Krishna.

Back to cricket in the World T-20 in October 2022. The Shane Warne mural in Melbourne was the first story we did. With colleagues who stood by me.

David Warner has always been a pillar of support. David and Candice Warner had come over to the hotel to meet up and we spent a fantastic time together. He even presented me with his World Cup shirt.

FIFA was another opportunity. We needed to diversify our coverage and the FIFA world cup was a platform.

Gopi yet again came to the Trailblazers conclave to lend a hand of support. His presence always made a difference.

The very best from Indian sport have been a part of the two editions of the Trailblazers conclave. Abhinav Bindra has always been a pillar of support and Neeraj Chopra has been a part of both editions of the conclave as was Adille Sumariwalla, President of Athletics Federation of India.

Sachin@50 was a product of love and I must acknowledge the support of fellow colleagues Kushan Sarkar, Arani Basu, Debasis Sen and Trisha Ghosal who worked on the book with me. It was hugely satisfying when Sunil Gavaskar agreed to be a part of it. Gulzaar saab wrote the piece for the back cover and Sachin Tendulkar launched the book in his house for his 50th birthday.

As Visiting Professor at the Neoma Business School in Paris in 2023, Professor Vijay Pereira and I have done some interesting work on sport and business and have also planned a conference in August 2024.

Team Revsportz has made a difference to the Indian sports eco-system with its coverage and passion. Proud to lead this dedicated bunch of journalists.

happened. But that didn't stop him filing factually incorrect and libellous matter. But Abhishek Kumar Singh is not the issue. He's just representative of a much deeper malaise—the mob-justice culture that overrides facts, something which compelled me to write this book.

I served my two-year ban. For him and others, I was just a trending story, one guaranteed to be read. Like a prop to boost your viewership as against quality work done. As a fellow journalist, did it even cross his mind that I might have told a few truths? But then, there would have been no story, or thousands of eyeballs. Writing against The Cricketer would have required a proper investigation, and a mind of one's own. But then, why bother when you could just join the troll army instead? *Behti Ganga mein haat dho lena.*

Such articles only strengthened my resolve though. I may have lacked the social media currency of an international cricketer, but no one could stop me taking refuge in my work. I knew I had to stay calm and focussed. The multiple trips to Birmingham helped me do just that.

I travelled to Birmingham three times between May and July 2022. The first trip, at the end of May, was to do a recce and record a few build-up shows for the Commonwealth Games. The second was in late June for the one-off Test match between England and India, and the third a fortnight or so later for the Commonwealth Games, which began on July 28. The work we did in Birmingham was the motivation I needed to get back into the zone. There was sporadic abuse on social media, but by June, I had become almost immune to it. With the cricket league over, The Cricketer was off the radar as well.

The June trip to Birmingham was from Dubai, where Pullela Gopichand had formally unveiled *Maverick Commissioner* at a very impressive gathering. Gopi had kept his word, and the event was a huge success. The launch was well covered, and the book got extremely good reviews in the media. I was in a good space as I boarded the flight to Birmingham. Thanks to another quirk of fate, Mayank Agarwal occupied the adjacent seat. He was on his way to join the Test squad in England. Mayank is another good acquaintance, and, in normal circumstances, we would have chatted all the way. But I was acutely conscious that the situation was anything but normal. The moment I realised that Mayank and I had seats next to each other on the Emirates flight, I requested the cabin crew to change my seat. It was natural that fans would come and seek autographs or pose for selfies with Mayank, and if I inadvertently appeared in the frame, there would be another backlash. It was best avoided, and I told Mayank why I was changing my seat. He was visibly uncomfortable, and asked me if things were okay.

The controversy had taught me a lot and one of the main lessons was to always be on guard. In public life, you must be careful. My messages, which had been used against me, were sent in a moment of frustration and disappointment. They had been misconstrued, and I had paid an unimaginable price. I was acutely aware that another false step during the ban period could push me straight back into the abyss.

On landing in Birmingham, Mayank needed a pound to get a luggage trolley for his cricket kit. He did not have any British currency on him. I got it for him and we had a laugh before we shook hands and he left for the team hotel. The circumstances meant that neither of us really felt comfortable, and it was the briefest of chats. My team was in Birmingham for the Test match, and we had big plans for the coverage. There were five of us at Edgbaston and no other Indian media house had such on-ground presence. While we were focussed on in-depth coverage, the plan was also to record a lot of the Commonwealth Games build-up shows on the side.

On the first morning of the Test match, I felt unusually anxious. I met Sir Geoff Boycott for breakfast at The Hyatt, and I remember him asking me where I was sitting at Edgbaston. Things had settled down a bit by then, but I kept asking myself how the trolls would react if I did cricket shows from outside the ground. Was it even prudent for me to go to the ground and do the pre- and post-match shows? Would it help Revsportz? I had bought hospitality tickets, but wasn't sure if going to the ground was a good idea. Eventually, I decided against it. So, while my teammates went to the stadium, I stayed back in the apartment and watched the game on the phone. It was strange, to say the least. I had come to Birmingham to cover the game, and was sitting alone in an apartment exactly five minutes from Edgbaston, watching the game on a small screen. I didn't go to the ground because I was scared, wary of yet more barbs directed at my family and me.

As I write this, I feel outraged. Part of me still thinks I should have gone to the ground and done all that was planned. The other side reckons what I did was right. I recorded a video when Rishabh Pant got his hundred, celebrating his effort. Within seconds of it going online, the faceless mob had started asking how I dared to cover Indian cricket when I was banned. They were determined not to let me work. The match was in the UK and not in India, and all I had done was post on my own platform. So, why the vitriol? But that's the nature of a media trial. It makes you question your sanity, eats into your well-being and pushes you to the brink. Just three months earlier, each interview I did was watched by hundreds of thousands of fans. Like I could do no wrong. And here, I was vilified like I was another person altogether. The realisation that social media is far too shallow and fickle had come to me a wee bit late.

While I did not go to Edgbaston, I did my shows from the city every evening. It was more of a travelogue about food than anything else, and it felt liberating. And because I had decided against going to Edgbaston to watch the game, I had a lot of free time during the day to work on a special show on Sourav Ganguly's 50th birthday on July 8. I had been invited to the birthday party in London, and I had decided not to go. Why go when I felt uncomfortable? With him, there was no formality and I told him exactly what I felt. He understood my point of view, and we agreed that it was the right thing to do.

While I did not attend the party, I was working on a slew of programmes for his birthday, for RevSportz and *Sangbad Pratidin*. For us in Bengal, it was an important occasion, and it was only natural that the Bengali media would plan something special. The Editor of *Sangbad Pratidin*, a dear friend of mine, was bringing out a special Sunday magazine celebrating Sourav, and the magazine's editor had called me to ask for a piece. I agreed, and was writing on Sourav's contribution to Indian cricket. Little did I know that there was a backstory to that as well. I was in Birmingham when The Editor called and told me, 'Sourav is perfectly fine with you writing on him.' My first thought was: 'Why shouldn't he be?' But I waited for him to continue. 'I hope you realise that it was important for me to tell him and be fully transparent,' he said. 'It is best for us all.' I could see what was being implied.

Within minutes, he called again. 'Could we do something really special for his birthday?' he asked. 'Something that will stand out.'

In normal circumstances, I would have requested Sachin Tendulkar to write something on Sourav, and it would have made for fantastic reading. But with very little time at hand, that wasn't a viable option. At the cost of digressing, it is important I state here that Sachin was one of the strongest pillars of support during my two wilderness years. He called multiple times to ask about my wellbeing, and repeatedly told me that all that mattered was my conscience. He said that life would challenge you on occasions, and only the strong stand up to that and prevail. When others stayed away or conveniently forgot, Anjali and Sachin were the first to call me on my birthday, within three weeks of the incident. They have always been there when I needed them.

As for the request from *Pratidin*, I thought what about Javed Akhtar Saab? How about requesting him to write a poem on Sourav, if he was agreeable? There could be nothing better than Javed Saab writing something for him. And for the Bengali press, it would be a coup. Having thought about the idea, I tried his number, which was switched off. When I woke up quite early the next morning, I decided to try again. Javed Saab picked up after one ring, and greeted me as warmly as always. I have always had tremendous respect and admiration for him, and was a little hesitant when I made my request. 'It is rather early here in London, so let me give it a thought and come back to you,' he told me. I was stunned. I had woken him up at 5:30 am my time thinking that he was in India, where it was 10 in the morning. I immediately apologised, and he started laughing. 'I came in last night, and am jetlagged,' said Javed Saab. 'I was up anyway.' On learning that I was in Birmingham, he asked if I could meet him in London that afternoon at around 3 pm. 'By then, I will have something ready for you,' he said.

I was delighted. Javed Saab penning something for Sourav would be a highlight. At a time when I was struggling for a break, it was the sort of thing that lifted the spirit. Javed Saab was in the city to watch Wimbledon, and I went to the Taj Residences in Central London at 3 pm with my teammates. Having heard of the meeting with Javed Saab, each was prepared to miss a day of the Test, and travel to London. As soon as we entered the apartment, Javed Saab made us feel at ease. 'I have written something for you,' he said. 'I am happy to recite it if you want. And if you like it, you can take the original for Sourav and use it.'

I asked him if we could record the recitation. Could this be the special RevSportz programme we had been looking for? In the absence of a renowned cricketer, we had to do something out of the box. Javed Akhtar reciting a poem for Sourav Ganguly on his birthday was just the kind of footage that would stand out.

Javed Saab agreed, and prefaced the recitation by saying that he was doing it because he had always had a special affection for me.

While doing the interview and listening to him, my eyes welled up and I could not speak. The hard work that I had put in over the past two decades did mean something after all. Nobody could discredit or make that body of work disappear, and this interview was yet more vindication. From Gopi to Javed Saab, the pieces were slowly moving back into place. Mentally, I was gradually getting back to where I needed to be.

Soon after we said our goodbyes to Javed Saab, I called those in *Pratidin* to tell them what I had gotten. Both sounded jubilant, and asked me to send the screenshot of the poem. They also wanted a written copy on the meeting and what had transpired. 'It will go as the lead,' said their Editor. At least the readers back home would associate my name with something different, after the derisory slander of the previous couple of months.

The Achinta Sheuli case

My team and I travelled to Birmingham for the third time in two months on July 25, to cover the Commonwealth Games, 2022. With the political class led by the Prime Minister taking an active interest in the contingent, there was a lot of buzz around the games. It was also the first occasion where fans were allowed in the stands after the Covid-19 pandemic.

As a storyteller who uses sport as a prism to make sense of life, the Commonwealth Games was a great opportunity. India would be watching, and my background and understanding of

Olympic sport gave me a head-start. If I was to rediscover my mojo, it would be during that fortnight.

One of the sports where India has traditionally done well at Commonwealth level is weightlifting, and under Vijay Sharma, the head coach, the performance graph had risen steadily. I had known him for years, and he was someone I had followed closely in an effort to map the weightlifting story. I reached out to Vijay ji soon after I reached Birmingham, to try and do some exclusive stories. Team India was training at a local gym, and as soon as I called Vijay ji on July 26, he asked me to go over and do the interviews. And in the course of the conversation, he singled out Achinta Sheuli and asked me to keep an eye on him. 'He is from your state, and is expected to win gold,' he told me. 'He is from a very humble background, and if you could help him in any way, it will make a real difference.'

I spoke to Achinta and made note of his event, since I was keen to see him perform. Very rarely does a Bengali athlete do well on the international stage. When they do, it is only natural that we, as fellow Bengalis, celebrate them. Achinta performed extremely well and won gold, exactly as Vijay ji had predicted. Soon after the win, RevSportz did an interview with him and put it on all our platforms. That chat went viral, and was widely picked up as well. I also spoke to one of my closest friends who is the India Head of Marketing for a global corporate giant that invests hugely in athletes and sportspersons. I asked if they could help Achinta in any way. This friend, a genuine sports aficionado, readily agreed and did so at the first available opportunity. In fact, the next time I met Achinta, he mentioned that he had already done a shoot with the same brand and was delighted about it.

Readers might wonder why am I writing about Achinta in particular? What relevance does it have to the broader story? Well, that's a fascinating tale in itself.

During the controversy, the one platform that hurled enormous abuse was the The Cricketer's Official 'fan club'. It was administered by an individual whose Facebook profile suggested that he was close to The Cricketer. He had made it a point to pepper me with invectives almost every single day between February and April 2022. In fact, the abuse continued for well over a year, abuse of a most personal kind including distortions of my name to suggest I was a criminal. In their (subscribers to the fan page) eyes, I was the reason for every misfortune that The Cricketer had ever encountered. So, when he wasn't included in the squad for the one-off Test at Edgbaston after a good cricket league in 2022, they trained their guns at me for his omission. While Team India's Head Coach and a top office bearer of the Apex Body were the two arch-villains of the piece, I was apparently responsible for influencing India's coach and the said office bearer against The Cricketer. With all those thousands of runs and over 100 international hundreds between them, they were dancing to a tune set by a journalist, apparently. Reason and logic had left the building long ago where these folk are concerned. That Facebook page makes for interesting reading, especially if you want to understand why the words 'social media' and 'cesspool' are now frequently interchangeable.

For the members of this fan club, every official within cricket's

Bengal body was a villain for their apparent mistreatment of The Cricketer. Each one is corrupt and a traitor. And several players in the then Indian side were 'quota player/s' who had made it to the team only because of their influence or the backing they had gotten from other influential players or other team members. Let's ignore that one of the youngest of these so-called 'quota' players has played two or three of the most extraordinary innings for India in overseas Test matches, and had the kind of impact that even the greatest players of the previous era did not. He was the architect of India's victory in Australia in 2021, having got his opportunity after The Cricketer failed in both innings in the first Test. But let's not allow facts to come in the way of a good conspiracy theory.

In all honesty, given the scale of this prodigy's performances, a comparison with The Cricketer is almost laughable. And yet, he was skewered almost daily for having taken his spot from The Cricketer. How he could have influenced selection, or what had he done, besides playing brilliantly, are inconvenient questions to ask members of this toxic fan club.

Many of them still hold me responsible for The Cricketer not being included in the team for the World Test Championship final in 2023. That I was banned in April 2022, and hadn't spoken to anyone in the selection committee for over a year was irrelevant. Even if I had been able to, the idea that I could coerce a panel of five into not considering a player is the stuff of a Neil Gaiman fantasy novel.

The language these fans used on a public platform was beyond the pale. But they continued to abuse with impunity because they knew there was no serious punishment for such behaviour. Unlike in the United Kingdom, where several fans have even been jailed for online abuse of athletes, India's justice system has yet to formulate or amend laws strong enough to take on such miscreants.

Soon after I posted a picture with Achinta celebrating his win, the fan club resumed its attack. Within minutes of the post, they had targeted my wife on her social media page, asking how I, a bully who had destroyed the career of Bengal's greatest cricketer, dared to interview another Bengali athlete. I apparently had no right to interview Achinta. Sharmistha was caught in the cross-hairs because I had posted a picture celebrating Achinta's medal, and told that we (RevSportz) had no business covering sport, having destroyed careers in the past. The irony of The Cricketer winning a cricket league title with his team *after* his career had been 'destroyed' (by me supposedly) clearly escaped them.

I tried to reason with the first few posts, but quickly gave up. You can't communicate with those driven only by hatred. And hatred for what? For things that I had no hand in? In fact, how many Indian sports fans still remember Achinta? Sadly, he did not win anything major since. And we had gone out of our way to help him. The slander continued for days, and the worst of it was often directed at my family. And while this so-called official fan club went about its daily vitriol, there was not a single public statement calling for restraint from The Cricketer. At the very least, he could have asked his loyal fans to refrain from such abuse and negativity on a platform that calls itself his Official Fan Club. We had to block and report a couple of dozen haters who (we cross-checked) were members of the said fan group, and vocal on the said social media page, and who had made it their business to heckle us constantly on social media, while we were covering the Commonwealth Games.

The Achinta incident was no aberration. Soon after Mirabai Chanu won her gold medal at these Games, we did an interview together over pizza. Chanu and I had known each other for a few years since the Tokyo Olympics. She loves pizza and, in an interview during the build-up to the Commonwealth Games, had asked me for pizza if she won. After winning the gold medal in style, and soon after she was finished with doping control, we met for a few minutes to celebrate the win. Chanu, I had argued in a newspaper article, was a symbol of a resurgent Northeast, which has produced a slew of champions in the last decade. That article was retweeted by the then Law Minister, who is himself from the region. The Minister had taken an active interest in sport since his time as Sports Minister in the Union Government. The piece had been well-researched and his retweet meant that it would be read by a wider cross-section of people. Within minutes of the retweet, however, there were comments slamming him for backing a bully, and one who was a 'disgrace for sport'. While The Minister, a seasoned politician, might not have taken such trolls seriously, it was disheartening to observe what went on.

The larger debate here should be about the impact of a social media trial. Over 99 per cent of those who write about you, dish out abuse or sit in judgement are far removed from the issue. They have no idea what happened and, typically, have Twitter profiles with between 0 and 1000 followers. In most cases, jumping on the bandwagon is an attempt to increase their social media currency. Sadly, abuse offers a short-cut. Rarely will you see these trolls post anything positive or constructive, unless it's to retweet a celebrity they dare not abuse. These icons have huge social media followings. These online squads, which call themselves Viratians and Rohitians, will stop at nothing should you say anything remotely critical of their idols. But isn't that a journalist's job—to do his work and call a spade a spade? The Cricketer's social media following rose by nearly 100,000 during the controversy. He was in the news and therefore popular. Each time he tweeted about being bullied and me having no remorse, the followers grew. I became easy prey, the soft target. And once you are designated as the enemy, the trolls will target you at every opportunity in a bid to stay relevant, like in the Achinta case. Whatever happened between The Cricketer and I had no bearing on a feature I had done on sport and the Northeast. Or an interview with Achinta. For this crowd, however, there was no nuance. They had, after all, labelled me a criminal. How could I be allowed to continue with my work? For them, my supposed crime was eternal. With social media platforms taking only half-hearted interest in removing this scourge, the trolls are emboldened to actually make a living from dishing out four-letter words and worse. Half of them may not even have heard of Mirabai Chanu, despite living in India, but that didn't stop them offering India's Law Minister advice.

I covered the Commonwealth Games without media accreditation. The process was on between February and April 2022, and with my life almost out of my control at the time, it had slipped my mind. I bought tickets for almost all events, and a friend who runs a sports tourism and experiential company—one of India's largest sports tourism and hospitality companies—helped me for the others. This meant that I did not have access to the mixed zone or the Main Press Centre, where athletes would come straight after their events to interact with the media. While this was a disadvantage, it was also an opportunity to see if my network was intact, and whether I would able to do stories of the kind I had done in the past. That's what brings me to P.V. Sindhu, the final anecdote in this chapter.

Sindhu was one athlete I had the privilege of covering from the time she was a star in the making. I was there at the Rio Olympics, in Tokyo and at multiple tour events, and had interacted with her dozens of times. In every sense, she was a friend and someone I had great regard and admiration for. As expected, Sindhu had made the final of the Commonwealth Games, and was one of India's most popular athletes in Birmingham. Without access to the mixed zone, I had not met or spoken to her during the event. An hour and a half after her gold-medal match, she had finished all her routine mixed-zone interactions and also gone through doping control. Most of the journalists had left the badminton hall and moved on to something else. Trisha and I were in the café just outside the venue when Sindhu walked in. She was alone and looking relaxed after winning the final. Seeing me there, she seemed surprised. 'I could see you in the gallery for all my games, and could hear you shout, but then I did not see you in the mixed zone,' she said with a smile. 'You don't want to interview me?' she joked. I told her why I had not been in the mixed zone. Without establishing contact on WhatsApp, usually frowned upon during tournaments, it had been impossible to get in touch. She heard me out patiently, and said: 'So, why don't we do something now? Outside the venue is perfectly fine to do something, and you wouldn't be breaking any media protocol either.'

Sindhu could sense I was taken aback. She smiled and said something that I remember quite vividly. 'If we could stay up till 3:10 am in Tokyo to do an interview, and if I could give you my Olympic-medal jersey, I hope you know I will always do whatever I can to help,' she said. 'You have done some fantastic work for Olympic sport, and helped me always.'

Before I could react, she said, 'Now, let's do it immediately, have to attend a number of things soon.'

We recorded the interview with her on the phone, and she was excellent as always. She spoke at length on what it felt like to see the tricolour go up, and the interaction was widely viewed and appreciated. The men and women who mattered had all stayed with me. The Commonwealth Games coverage was a spectacular success, and we were clawing back on lost ground.

However, I had not done much cricket work since the controversy. That would be the acid test. Would there be takers for my work, or would the high priests of social media have the final say?

The T20 World Cup in Australia would give me the answer.

8
World T20 in Australia

The T20 World Cup in Australia was the first major cricket tournament I reported on after the ban. Firstly, it wasn't in India. Second, it was played six months after the sanction was imposed, a fair amount of time for people to move on to other issues and villains. I was also far more confident after a hugely successful Commonwealth Games. It was about self-belief more than anything else, and I was determined that the trolls wouldn't faze me. If the abuse started up again, I was resilient enough to get through it.

The big question that I had to confront was whether I should travel to Australia. The safer option was to work on the tournament from the studio. Debasis and another colleague, a senior journalist, who is based out of Mumbai, and who had come on board for the World Cup, were both travelling, and we had our Australian colleague on ground in Melbourne. Even if I did not go, we had enough on-ground presence to put out some excellent stories. But then, why would I stay away? We had sponsors on board for the World Cup and I owed it to them not to take the easy option. I applied for accreditation because it was a global event and under the aegis of the ICC.

Having said that, I wasn't sure I would be accredited. What had once been a routine procedure before the sanctions was now an uncertain process, and I bought hospitality tickets as a back-up plan. I was aware that the controversy might force the ICC to play safe.

It was at the end of August that I got a call from one of my friends within the ICC's senior management. There had been a discussion on the matter, and they had decided to accredit me. They felt I had an unblemished record, and had done some very good work in the past. There was also no formal communication from India requesting that they do anything to the contrary. However, I was told to consider if I wanted to use the accreditation. Might being in the press box trigger a backlash, which could then impact RevSportz's coverage? If I could largely do my work using the hospitality tickets, why take a chance?

There was merit in that argument. Even if there was one social media post questioning my presence in the media enclosure, it could trigger immediate and nasty reactions. While I wasn't unduly worried about sticks and stones hurled, I knew that such tirades would deflect attention away from the hard yards that our team would be putting in down under. The prudent option was to not use the accreditation. I informed the ICC of my decision well in advance, so that they would accredit someone else. The RevSportz plan was for Debasis to be in the press box, while I would buy my passage into the venues. Nothing stopped me from writing after watching matches from the stands. Filming from inside the venue was anyway not an option since we were not rights holders. It was the right decision under the circumstances.

The Twitter series

Just before the World Cup, a friend and the content lead at Twitter India, reached out to me with a proposal. Saudi Tourism wanted to do a five-part series around the tournament, and I was asked if I wanted to be a part of that. They mostly wanted local colour stories, and it would be an interesting series to be a part of during the World Cup. Based on the plan, I decided to do my first story in Melbourne on a Shane Warne mural, painted in his honour in St Kilda shortly after he tragically passed away in March 2022. It was a good story with which to set the tone for the coverage. The morning after we landed, the team went to St Kilda. It took us a few minutes of fumbling around before we found the small by-lane where the mural was located. Interestingly, the man who had painted it was in the house, and agreed to speak to us on camera. It was a fascinating story. The Twitter people were extremely pleased with the idea, and the collaboration was off to a great start.

Or so I thought.

Soon after the story was published on my handle and promoted by Twitter, the blowback began. How dare Twitter work with a banned journalist, and promote his work? Why had

I travelled to Melbourne to cover cricket, and why was it being endorsed by Twitter? Many of the messages were just rants not even worth a second glance.

Twitter, however, had to take a call. Did they want to continue with the series, or would the negativity it might spawn be too much to deal with? With new ownership in place, they were in an uncomfortable situation.

Within a few hours, I got the call. 'I am sure you have seen the reaction,' he told me. 'It is wrong, but we just need to be a little smart. First, we will absolutely continue with the series. But just for the time being, try and minimise your presence on screen. Let's go step by step.'

What he said made absolute sense to me. This wasn't the time for bravado. To use a cricket analogy, I was batting in the first hour of a game, and had to respect the bowlers and the conditions. After lunch, with the sun out, there would be enough time to step out and play a few shots.

The next few videos we did used a lot more footage, and I was hardly visible on screen. We got good traction, and the series was very well executed. Sadly, the said friend at Twitter was one of the many who lost his job in the reshuffle, and we couldn't celebrate the success of the series together. That said, I remain indebted to him for his advice.

The India-Pakistan blockbuster

October 23, 2022 was a historic day. India vs Pakistan is always special, and this time round, India came into the game on the back of a rare World Cup defeat to Pakistan at the previous

World T20 in Dubai. While words like 'revenge' have no place in sport, settling scores was very much on Indian minds heading into the contest. At the Asia Cup in Dubai a few weeks earlier, the two matches between the great rivals had been split. Some reckoned that this particular game could attract over 100,000 people to the Melbourne Cricket Ground and break the existing record of 100,024 spectators. The eventual turnout was just over 91,000, though the tinder-box atmosphere both sets of fans created made you wonder if there were considerably more.

For every journalist, this was the game to cover. It made for great stories, both print and visual. Because I did both, there was much to be done. But then, what would things be like at the MCG, and would I be comfortable? Every Indian journalist would be working in the same area. It would be the first time since the controversy that I was seeing a number of colleagues from the fraternity. I was excited and anxious at the same time. I knew that I could not lose my cool. I had heard a lot of what was said about me, and it was important to keep a lid on my emotions.

The MCG was a spectacle. Mostly blue with a sprinkling of green, it had dressed up for the occasion. The cricket world was back on its feet after the Covid-19 pandemic, and this was the ultimate proof that things were back on track. I reached the MCG about two hours before the game, and could feel the sense of anticipation. I have always loved and enjoyed working on the field. At that moment, the ban, trolls and abuse were far from my thoughts. I was in Australia to try and do some quality work, and little else mattered.

Almost everyone I knew walked up to greet me. And no one referred to the controversy until a longstanding friend, came up and asked jokingly: 'So how is it to lead the life of a banned journalist?' For a second, I was in two minds. Did he actually say it in jest, or was he trying to provoke me? But before I could say anything, he cleared the air. 'Your Commonwealth Games coverage was fantastic,' he said. 'I am very pleased you did all of it from Birmingham.'

The speaker is a good journalist, and was in Melbourne without accreditation. In a sense, we intended to cover the tournament in similar ways, and we discussed our ideas at some length. We planned to sit down for a longer chat and explore opportunities to work together. RevSportz was set up with the idea of getting several experienced and enthusiastic journalists under one umbrella. For the longest time, sports had been treated as a silo in the news media business. When even the Prime Minister used sport extensively to get his messages across, it was still one bulletin in the primetime band on most television platforms. Many, in fact, did not do regular sports bulletins anymore. Some media companies have stopped sending sports journalists to events, preferring to cover key tournaments off television.

How is Neeraj Chopra winning a Diamond League competition not a news event? Who decides that it is not relevant enough to merit on-ground coverage? With RevSportz, we wanted to be disruptors who were on location at every major event. It is a platform for sports journalists and the said journalist fit the bill. A conversation was in order.

Immediately after I finished the pre-match show and was about to make my way into the hospitality stand through Gate 6, I spotted a colleague from my previous organisation, who now heads sport for that same media house. He was still doing his show and, for a few fleeting seconds, we made eye contact. He had always been respectful in person, and we nodded at each other. For nearly a decade, we had covered World Cups together. This was the first one since I had moved on to set up RevSportz. He was still on air, and I didn't think there would be an opportunity to speak. That was when I saw him take a few steps towards me. My RevSportz colleague from Mumbai was there as well. 'Ab hamare saath yahan hamare do karibi dost bhi jud gaye hain [Two of our close friends have joined us here],' said this former colleague on air, and seemed about to pull me into his frame. Maybe he was unnerved by the chance meeting, and emotions got the better of him. While my RevSportz colleague was clearly surprised, I politely pushed his hand aside and walked away.

He could have extended the hand of support when the controversy erupted. After all, he knew me better than most. He could perhaps have checked the actions of another journalist that worked with him, and who had pressured a colleague of mine to speak against me. Instead, he decided to stay silent. I have already recounted that a journalist that worked in sport for the same media house had repeatedly called Debasis when the controversy had erupted, causing Debasis immense discomfiture. While it is not too much to ask a former colleague to join you on your show in a spirit of banter, I was no longer comfortable being on this show. It represented for me a past that I did not wish to revisit. We have exchanged messages since, and been in touch now and then.

As we walked towards the gate, we met a young Indian couple who looked rather flustered. My RevSportz colleague spoke to them in Marathi and learned that they had come to Australia for their honeymoon, and hoped to watch the India-Pakistan game. On landing in Melbourne, they became aware that the game was sold out and it was almost impossible to organise tickets at the eleventh hour. 'We are huge cricket fans, and the reason we came here was to watch this game,' the husband told us. 'With the MCG capacity close to 100,000, we felt it wouldn't be an issue to buy tickets. Had we known this would be the situation, we would have bought tickets long back.'

'This was to be my gift to him,' said his wife. As I listened to them, it struck me that these were the kind of fans who made Indian cricket what it is. Without such fans, there would be no cricket league, for example. And now, they would have to head back to Mumbai without fulfilling their dream of watching cricket's marquee match-up. The friend that runs one of the leading sports tourism companies in India, was an official agent of the ICC. On the spur of the moment, I called him and asked if he had two tickets to give me. I was happy to pay, but I knew he was unlikely to accept the money. 'These are the last few tickets, so if you badly need them, please take,' he said. 'I am sending you two tickets.'

I asked the couple to wait for a few minutes, so that we could work something out. Just then, my friend sent me the two tickets he had promised on my WhatsApp. I was delighted to offer them to the couple as a wedding present. They looked stunned. 'How much should we pay you?' asked the husband. 'We can pay you any amount you want,' said his wife. 'This is incredible.' When I told them it was a gift and that they need not pay anything, they did something strange. The husband suddenly touched my feet, and sought my blessings. 'We don't know how to thank you,' said his wife, almost in tears. 'You do not even know us, and yet you have just given us our best wedding present.' It was an incredibly satisfying feeling to see them float away as though on a cloud. Sport is all about spreading positivity, and I sent a long thank-you note to my friend for the tickets, before going into the ground.

I met them again at the end of the match, while rushing to do my show. We had just witnessed a Virat Kohli innings for the ages, and the husband gave me a warm hug before saying: 'If we can ever do anything for you, we would be grateful.'

Those words made India's win sweeter still.

Sunil Gavaskar and Michael Clarke

The night before the India-Pakistan game, the sports tourism company run by the friend who had so kindly sent me these tickets, had organised a chat show for their clients with Sunil Gavaskar and Michael Clarke, at the Melbourne Skydeck. They had done similar programmes in the past. During the 2019 World Cup in the UK, I had hosted all of them, which were then edited and broadcast on Star Sports. Sunny bhai and Michael are both very close to me, and I wasn't surprised that I was asked to host the function. 'Yahan toh tum kar hi sakte ho [Here, you can do it],' my friend told me. 'You must.' While I was touched by his faith in me, I wasn't sure if Sunny bhai and Michael would be comfortable. I asked him to check with them, just to be sure there would be no awkwardness on the day. Both men agreed, and it was hugely enjoyable to host a very good build-up event on the eve of such a massive game.

We had a great session, which gave me plenty of material and insight for my written pieces. While Sunny bhai had a contract with an Indian media house, Michael was commentating on the World Cup for the ICC. He did not have a contract with an Indian publication or broadcaster, and I could, in theory, ask him to do an interview for RevSportz. In the decade and a half that we had known each other, Michael had never said no to me. Yet, I wasn't sure. He had not brought up the issue, and I had not had a chance to explain matters to him. That said, he was certainly aware of the ban. Michael was waiting for the audience to click a few photographs after the event finished, and in a hurry to leave for a dinner engagement. That was when I asked if I could have a word.

'I was waiting for you to say this,' he said with his usual grin. 'I did not want to mention it and make you uncomfortable. Of course, mate, let's go to the other end of the room and sit and chat for a few minutes.' After a pause, he went on: 'Listen, mate. We all go through shit in life. Things just don't go to plan. But that does not mean it will impact our friendship. You and I have always been friends, and that's what defines us. If you want an interview for your channel, just go ahead and take it. I will stay back and do it.'

I called Debasis over, and asked him to record what would be my first proper cricket interview since the sanctions were imposed. It was perhaps fitting that it was a conversation with Michael. Just ahead of the 2015 World Cup, Michael, then captain of Australia, was desperately trying to get fit in time to play the tournament. He wasn't going through the best of times. After the world of cricket lost Phil Hughes in November 2014, Michael had struggled both physically and mentally. Hughes had been one of the players closest to him, and for the longest time, the wallpaper on his mobile phone was a picture of them together. He was injured during the second Test against India, and ruled out of the series. Yet another surgery meant that his World Cup participation was in doubt.

That was when Michael and I became close. I used to call him almost every single day, just to offer words of support and encouragement. We would speak about Hughes, how fickle life was, and how important the World Cup was for him. By then, he knew it would be his final year in international cricket, and he wanted to push his body for that one final challenge. Not once did I ask him for an interview or comment. We were just friends, and neither of us used that to ask for any kind of favours. Just ahead of the World Cup, Michael had called to ask if I would be travelling to Australia. I would be covering the tournament for the media house I then worked for, in my capacity as Consulting Editor, Sports. That was when he asked if I wanted to do a long interview. He had not spoken to a single journalist in months, and was the most sought-after interview in world cricket at the time. 'I will keep aside an hour for you,' he told me. 'Just come and we will do something nice together.' True to his word, we met at the Langham in Melbourne, and it was one of the best interviews I have done.

Both of us remembered that, and Michael referred to it. 'During the 2015 World Cup, mine was the first interview you did,' he said with a chuckle. 'It's the same seven years later.'

Michael made my evening, and ensured that RevSportz's coverage in Australia got off to a rocking start.

Soon after the interview was over, Debasis, another colleague and I decided to rush back to our apartment—the Adina next to Federation Square—to send the footage to the team in India. It was a big exclusive, and we needed to get it edited and online as quickly as possible. But there was a traffic jam next to the Flinders Street Station, and we jumped out of the taxi to walk across to the hotel. Just as we approached the Adina, we saw Mohammed Siraj coming out of Desi Dhaba, one of the better Indian restaurants in the Melbourne CBD. Desi Dhaba had partnered with us for our World Cup coverage, and I had known the owners for a while. The food there was excellent, and it was no surprise that Siraj had chosen to visit to try some Indian fare. He was someone I had done quite a few interviews with in the past. One of the simplest and hardest-working players in the team, he is fantastic for the sport. Siraj greeted me warmly the moment we saw each other, and asked if I wanted to come in and have some food. He did so out of politeness, but within seconds, I was acutely aware of the situation. Had someone clicked a picture and posted it on social media, the Justice-for-The Cricketer brigade would have a field day. I had already paid a heavy price, and couldn't afford another false step. And Siraj, the warmest of individuals, certainly didn't deserve to be caught in the crossfire. I thanked him for the offer, and continued on to the hotel.

What mattered was that Siraj greeted me without a trace of discomfort, and the relationship was unchanged. In the circumstances, that was much more important than a shared meal.

Diwali in Sydney

Sydney, much like New York, is one of the world's most breath-taking cities. The pace and buzz make it a favourite of mine, and I was thrilled that we were there for Diwali. Harris Park, the desi hub, could compete with any neighbourhood back home, and we made elaborate arrangements to celebrate and showcase that to our viewers. The plan was to have lunch at Harris Park and a celebratory dinner at Masala Theory, one of my favourite restaurants in the Sydney CBD. We had informed Yashpal Erda, the owner, much in advance, and booked a table for six at 8:30 pm. Each of us had decided to wear kurta-pajama that evening, and had requested some special dessert to mark the occasion. We were to be picked up from the hotel at 8 pm, and I was just getting ready to go down to the lobby when Yashpal called. 'The Indian players are all coming for dinner,' he told me. 'I just thought I should let you know in case you want to do something. Or if you want to come slightly later. Just thought it was important you know.'

Yashpal and I had known each other for six years, and he

had always been a well-wisher. He knew it could get awkward if we were all seated in the same space, and had called to inform me. I requested him to move the booking to 9:30 pm, since the players were expected to leave by then. And it was only after 9:15 pm that we started out for Surry Hills, where Masala Theory is located.

Yashpal greeted us at the entrance, and said that some of the players were still there. But he had arranged a table for us outside, and asked that we make ourselves comfortable. It was all elaborately laid out, and the food was amazing. It started to rain just as we were about to finish the main course, and move to dessert. In the next few minutes, the drizzle became a heavy shower. I had my back to the entrance, and couldn't see that Suryakumar Yadav and Rishabh Pant were standing there. They were waiting for a taxi.

That was when Surya said: 'Arre, Dada, is it you? Kahan ho aap, mile nahi? [Hello, brother, is it you? Where are you? Haven't met?]' He had heard my voice. Only when I stood up and turned around did I see them. Surya was all smiles on seeing me. We all wished each other happy Diwali, and I also congratulated him on becoming the world's No. 1-ranked T20 batter. He was in exceptional form and was India's go-to batter in the competition. We spoke for a few minutes, and Rishabh was polite enough to click pictures with some of my colleagues. That was when I casually told Surya that he shouldn't stand there and speak to me for too long, because it could land both of us in trouble. He squirmed a bit then, but recovered his poise soon enough. 'Dada, all will be well,' he said, before giving me a warm hug. It was a good end to the Diwali meal, and we left for the hotel after wishing the players the best for the World Cup.

Perth

India played South Africa in Perth. That was always going to be a tricky game. The pitch had pace and bounce, and South Africa, with Kagiso Rabada, Lungi Ngidi and Anrich Nortje, posed some serious challenges for the Indian batting line-up. To add to the Indians' discomfort, it was extremely cold in Perth. Even the locals said it was unnaturally cold, and woollen jumpers and jackets used in the peak of winter had to be brought out.

In Perth, Norman, our Australian colleague, introduced me to Alan Mullaly, the former England fast bowler. He is now a resident, and a warm gentleman. Absolutely no airs about him, and he took us to his house and made some chicken curry. Alan, who stays with his mother, became a friend. We decided to go to the game together, and it was most instructive to have Alan speak to us about Arshdeep Singh. Having seen Alan with us, a few others from the Indian media had reached out to him, asking for interviews.

On match day, Alan dropped myself and a colleague at the Optus Stadium, and drove off to park his car. With time on our hands, we decided to record a few videos of the fans trooping in. Such clips tend to do well on digital platforms, and add a certain flavour to the overall coverage. As we were recording, I spotted Kushan and a few known faces from the fraternity, other journalists. I asked them if they wanted to record a segment analysing the game. One of them, Abhishek Tripathi, a very good sports reporter, immediately agreed, and we recorded a very interesting and funny snippet together. The said journalist, who had only rarely spoken to me before that, was extremely supportive, and since Perth, we have become friends. We have not only discussed stories and exchanged notes, but also met socially and had a few meals together. Abhishek has in fact called me on multiple occasions since then and said he is there to help in anyway possible. He knows what had happened and has forever said that whatever happened with me was wrong.

In fact, in the few weeks in Australia I spent some happy moments with fellow colleagues like Abhishek, Kushan, Debasis, Amit Shah and Sandipan Banerjee. With Abhishek Tripathi and Kushan we celebrated their birthday together and I cooked for both on what turned out to be a great evening of cricket conversations. These occasions gave me a sense of solidarity with my professional peers that I thought I had lost. I will always look back to these moments with fondness.

Sydney and the Pakistan semi-final

While India played England in the Adelaide semi-final, Pakistan were pitted against New Zealand in Sydney. I was keen for RevSportz to do on-ground coverage of both semi-finals, and decided to send Debasis to Adelaide. I travelled to Sydney. Against the odds, Pakistan played some fantastic cricket and beat Kane Williamson's New Zealand to make the final. Soon after the match ended, the SCG was a sight to behold. Pakistani fans were out there in numbers celebrating, and each was keen to see an India-Pakistan final. The Pakistan media was well-represented, and seeing me do my videos outside the SCG with a colleague, quite a few came up and said hello. Some even asked if I would be part of their shows. It was a very happy and vibrant atmosphere. I did quite a few 'live' clips for RevSportz, and just as we were wrapping up, a group of journalists walked up and asked if things were okay with me. The question came out of the blue, and disconcerted me.

'We followed every single detail of what happened, and felt the reaction was over the top,' said one. 'How can you be banned for two years for sending that message?' Another was even more blunt. 'The player played you,' he said. 'He was dropped from the team, and it was the right time to put out the tweet. Had he done so at any other time, no one would take notice.'

'If the date was blurred out, why did you not point it out earlier?' asked a third person. Shahid Hashmi, one of the most senior and respected Pakistani journalists, told me, 'Bhai, just do your work. What is important for us is to do our work. Everything else will take care of itself.' Hashmi is now a consultant at Revsportz.

We agreed to meet for dinner later that night, and I remember a rasmalai party in my apartment, the Meriton on Danks Street. We were all optimistic about the possibility of an India-Pakistan final, and made elaborate plans to meet in Melbourne the following day. Little did we know that Jos Buttler and Alex Hales would smash India out of the competition.

As Shahid bhai and the other Pakistani journalists left for their hotels, I was left to wonder why these men understood what had gone on, while those I had worked shoulder-to-shoulder with in India did not. How was it that they saw through the motive, when almost no one in India questioned it? Was it because we weren't competitors, and I was no threat to these other journalists? How did professional competition become stiffer than the brotherhood one had shared?

With no answers to be found, it was best to let things be.

The return flight

With India out of the tournament, there was no point in me staying back for the final. My colleagues were both there, and could finish RevSportz's coverage of the tournament. I was homesick, and managed to advance my return to November 12, giving me two extra days at home. The return flight was from Sydney, and just as I was about to enter the lounge, I spotted a senior corporate leader whom I had met a few times in the past. His company invests serious money in cricket, and he too was heading back with India no longer in the fray. 'For how long will we choke in high pressure games?' he asked me. 'You should write about it. Unless you win ICC tournaments, how is it that you are the best in the world? If you are playing team sport, it is not enough that you score runs. You need to win it for your team. That's the only relevant thing.'

Having spoken like any disappointed fan, he then turned his attention to my predicament. 'I hope your situation is all under control at the moment,' he said. 'The Cricketer was acting with a kind of entitlement knowing that the Apex Body would be forced to protect him. How does anyone know who was telling the truth?'

I was enjoying the conversation. He was saying what I had all along, but it was satisfying to hear those words from someone else for a change. 'Did anyone try reaching out to you?' he asked. 'I think you just happened to be a pawn who was used.'

While that could well be the case, the price I had to pay for being a chess piece was a very heavy one. Disappointed as I was that India had squandered another opportunity to win an ICC trophy, I was satisfied with the work RevSportz had done in Australia. India may have lost, but I had taken important steps on the road back. I was doing cricket work, and enjoying it once again. The sporadic online outbursts no longer stung, and that was the biggest positive I took home from that trip to Australia. It was time to test myself again. With that in mind, I watched Abhishek Bachchan's *Guru* one more time on the way home!

9

Conclave and *Sachin@50*

One of my biggest fears in February-March 2022 centred on what would happen if our sponsors at RevSportz decided to walk away. With all the negative publicity on social media, I couldn't fault anyone for saying that it wasn't in their best interest to work with me at the time. That only one of our twelve partners bailed out was perhaps the best boost we could have got.

'We have been associated with you for years now, and we know what you stand for,' said the CEO of one of the companies that had stood steadfast in their support of both me and RevSportz. 'If you take a look at my inbox, you will find many similar messages that I have sent to friends. It is normal that you will be relaxed with friends, and not always be politically correct. To say it was a threat was outrageous.' They continued to back the show, *Backstage With Boria,* and it has only gotten bigger and better over time. And along the way, we have added a number of new brands to our list of partners, and each of them has enabled us to further serve Indian sport with quality multi-discipline content.

After what had happened, it was important to do something different from the day-to-day to get back some positive energy. We needed to vindicate the faith the sponsors had shown. Something that would make us stand apart and showcase the effort we put in round the year. Something that could help reposition the RevSportz brand, and move a step ahead of the controversy. That was how we zeroed in on planning India's biggest-ever Sports Conclave. With Olympic and Paralympic sport on the rise, and with India taking strides towards becoming a multi-sport nation, it was important to get the best athletes under one roof to celebrate the growth story. It would also be consistent with our vision of doing optimal coverage across every major Olympic sport. Hardly ever had it happened that 25 of India's best athletes, across sports, had come together to share their narratives on one platform. To manage the logistics, get the dates aligned and ensure that there was cohesiveness among the panels was a huge challenge. But then, if you want to do something different, you need to be prepared for some hard yards. And now we have done it a second year as well. Bigger and better.

The plan was made in a rather fortuitous manner. I had a passport renewal appointment in December 2022, a month after returning from Australia, and had forgotten my original BA marksheet at home. The marksheet was now a mandatory requirement at the Passport Office, and I requested a colleague to bring it while I waited at the passport office in Anandapur in Kolkata. The T20 World Cup in Australia and the FIFA World Cup in Qatar soon after had given me the confidence to step on the accelerator. We needed to build on that momentum. That's when the idea of the conclave first came to me. With most elite sportspersons training on their own, there was no forum where they could meet and exchange ideas. There were some awards functions, but little meaningful dialogue is possible during a two or three-hour function. We needed athletes, corporates, policy-makers and the media to come together. That's when something meaningful would happen. With the Olympics cycle on, it was important to map the progress of each discipline that India was banking on. After the relative high of the Tokyo Olympics, the fraternity needed to take stock and re-evaluate goals.

But then, a conclave on this scale would involve serious monies, and we needed to get a lot of things in order. Could we get all the best athletes under one roof for a day and a half? Could we get funding? What about the venue and publicity? In the one and a half hours that I sat idle at the passport office, I made a number of calls to athletes to gauge their interest in the idea. They needed to be there in person to make the conclave meaningful, and after about 10 calls, I was convinced this was a must-do project. Each of the athletes I spoke to felt it could be a very important platform for dialogue. Some like Abhinav Bindra and Gopichand suggested that I should try and do it annually. Not one referenced the cricket controversy. On the way home, I went to the ITC Royal Bengal, which had the biggest banquet hall in the city, and made a booking for March 8, 2023. It was International Women's Day, and there was no better occasion to speak of and celebrate empowerment narratives in sport.

I wanted to document how sport helped change lives, and reached out to Abhinav to come and speak on the Olympic Value Education Programme (OVEP) in Odisha, which now includes more than 150,000 young children from relatively underprivileged backgrounds. Abhinav's Foundation steers the project, and it has brought about real on-ground change. We invited Gopi and Vijay Sharma, the chief weightlifting coach, to talk about the fundamentals of coaching, and how to manage superstars like Sindhu and Mirabai Chanu. We invited Neeraj Chopra—who could well be regarded as India's best-ever athlete if he wins in Paris—and Nikhat Zareen to share their stories with younger, aspiring athletes in the audience. We would have Deepa Malik and Devendra Jhajharia talking about the Paralympic growth story. Vinesh Phogat and Sakshi Malik, faces of the wrestlers' protest, agreed to come and speak about why change was necessary. In no time, we had the best of Indian sport agreeing to be present. They were all people that I had known for years through my work, people who I had interviewed on multiple occasions, and who responded instantly. And yet again, no one asked me a single question about the ban, or what my plans were with respect to cricket. Eventually, we had to advance the date of the conclave to March 5, because March 8 happened to be Holi.

By the time we announced the conclave, we had Tata Steel on board as presenting partner. Given the contributions of the Tata Group towards promoting Indian Olympic sport, there could be no better brand synergy. When I explained the idea behind the conclave to Mr T.V. Narendran, the Managing Director of Tata Steel, and Chanakya Chaudhuri, Senior Vice President and Head of Corporate Services, they did not take too much time to confirm their support. The plan came together seamlessly.

Soon after news of the conclave became public, the murmurs began. Posts did the rounds on Twitter and Facebook, which asked how elite athletes could come to a conclave that I was putting together. How could I, a 'banned journalist' who had 'bullied and threatened' and 'tried to finish the life of a cricketer', still work in sport and organise an event on this scale?

Some advised Neeraj, Abhinav, Nikhat and Mira to not speak to me, for I was 'evil'. Others reacted with remarks like '*Phir interview maang raha hai, sharm nahi hai iss aadmi mein?* [Again asking for interviews, this man has no shame?]', while the more creative offered up thoughtful gems like: '*Teri maa-ki, chup rahe BSDK*'.

I was angry and deeply frustrated. These self-styled moral arbiters knew nothing of what had happened, yet that didn't stop them hurling abuse from the safety of unverified or anonymous handles. A conclave that could enrich the Indian sports narrative meant nothing to these trolls who live their lives wading every day through the negativity on social media. For them, every negative comment is the chance to garner some followers, because nothing gets more eyeballs than cuss words and hate—such is the reality of our times. Most are perhaps frustrated with their own lives and social media is a platform to vent some of these frustrations.

I knew this was what a media trial entailed—guilty till proven innocent. My every action would be attacked. Maligned and trolled, with hardly anyone from my fraternity coming forward to support me.

I was taunted on an almost daily basis—the conclave would fail miserably, no athletes would attend, kept away by my pack of lies. They went as far as to write to the International Olympic Committee (IOC), asking them not to associate with me. An email was sent to Abhinav, suggesting that he would be doing a disservice to Indian sport by attending the conclave. The bottom line was clear—I should not be allowed to work. I should suffer. How could it be business as usual? If I could organise a conclave, what was the point of the ban?

Frankly, there also was a sense of resignation in some of these messages. These individuals had wanted to trample me into the dust. They could not digest that I was fighting back. How could I? After what I had (allegedly) done, how could I have a career in sport? How could the social media trial NOT be the last word? How could the troll army NOT be the arbiters of people's fates? How could the herd of these faceless and nameless entities be made to feel any less powerful? How could I be allowed to win?

Not one of these self-appointed moral guardians had ever considered the possibility that I was not lying. Not one stopped to doubt The Cricketer for even one instant. That it was one man's word against the other's. Yet, even they would wonder why there had been no consequences for his astonishing outburst against the establishment on social media before he had branded me a bully. I had told the committee the truth, including the circumstances leading to me sending my poorly worded message.

I could have gone in for a compromise and weaselled my way out of trouble, as so many had advised me to do. But I didn't. Instead, I had dared to call out The Cricketer.

The conclave, much to the dismay of the troll army, was a resounding success. It's no exaggeration to say that it was the best sports conclave India had ever seen. The evidence lay in the tweets from athletes who had all been delighted to be part of the event, and who hoped that it would continue year on year. For a young Manu Bhaker to listen to Abhinav Bindra speak about handling pressure, and how he went about training, was a real lesson. For each aspiring Olympic athlete, Abhinav remains a role model. In between sessions, many like Mehuli Ghosh went and discussed topics with Abhinav. A group of Bengal shuttlers discussed the finer aspects of their sport with Gopi, and, for the first time, younger athletes could see legends like Anju Bobby George, Deepa Malik, Joshna Chinappa, Rani Rampal, Deepika Kumari and Mirabai Chanu discuss each other's careers and what sport had taught them.

With almost every athlete tweeting or writing about the conclave, the negative discourse was gradually drowned out. If the athletes took away such positive vibes from the event, how indeed could the naysayers respond? While some tried to mock me with references to 'Ypu', the hate campaign seemed to slowly be running out of puff. Others tried to get under the skin by being cheeky. Comments on the lines of 'You should call The Cricketer' or 'Why is The Cricketer not in the conclave?' were posted every now and then. But in the days following the conclave, it was hard to find much negativity. There was one caveat, however. Anything remotely critical of players like Virat and Rohit in the aftermath of the World Test Championship final, and the filth would start again. The ban would be cited, and I would be reminded of my place as someone who had been stopped from reporting on Indian cricket. By that stage, however, I had long stopped caring.

The conclave, which saw a significant number of India's Olympic icons in Kolkata—a couple did their sessions over Zoom—was the biggest possible vindication that nothing could come in the way of hard effort. No troll will ever win in the face of quality work. As Abhinav, who I count as a friend, likes to say, it was sport that taught him how to lose, how to deal better with life's challenges, and how to make a difference. I came to the same realisation, as the ban imposed on me taught me how to handle the lowest moments while staying resilient. As much as life knocked you down, you could always get back up with renewed confidence in your ability. It showed me how deep I could dig, to discover inner steel that I did not know existed. When my family was targeted and even my daughter abused, I found that strength from somewhere, anywhere. The controversy had made me both mentally stronger and better at what I did. By all counts, a better version of myself.

Sachin@50

Sachin Tendulkar turned 50 on April 24, 2023. As his biographer, it was only natural that I would want to do something meaningful to mark the occasion. I had the privilege of hosting his 40th birthday celebrations in Kolkata in 2013, and was keen to make the 50th memorable for one of my favourite athletes of all time.

Sachin, I have to say, is much more than a sportsperson for me. I first came upon his name at the age of 11. The year was 1987. As a child who had grown up with cricket, it was inevitable that I mourned Sunil Gavaskar's retirement. Almost overnight, Indian cricket was in need of a new saviour. Dilip Vengsarkar was in great form, Sanjay Manjrekar had a seemingly watertight technique and Mohammad Azharuddin had magic wrists. But truth be told, none of the three was in the league of the just-retired Gavaskar. It was then that I read about Tendulkar in a Mumbai newspaper—a child prodigy touted as Indian cricket's next big thing.

Then came his debut series in Pakistan. It was terrifying to think of how a boy of 16 would stand up to the likes of Imran Khan, Wasim Akram and Waqar Younus—the jet-speed debutant. My worst fears came true in the Sialkot Test, when Tendulkar was hit on the nose by a Waqar scorcher. He had blood all over his face, but not once did he think of leaving the field. Watching him continue to bat, and then cream one through cover for four, I realised that the saviour Indian cricket had been waiting for had arrived, with a teenager's face and a Zen master's composure.

By the mid-1990s, Sachin had become my hero, a singular icon that Indian cricket fans would follow to every corner of the globe. But it was the 1999 World Cup that brought to light his unrivalled commitment to the nation. Having returned home after his father's demise, Tendulkar was back in action within days. His look up at the sky after completing a fantastic hundred against Kenya—a century he dedicated to his father—brought tears to the eyes of millions of cricket fans.

For many like me, who grew up in an India that had fallen prey to turmoil and secessionist movements, he was a ray of hope, helping to carve out a national image that was solid and resolute. He was a sign of India's resurgence, the quiet reassurance that things were bound to get better.

In the first Test played on Indian soil after the 26/11 terror attack in 2008, it was imperative that the team played well to get the country back to a feeling of normalcy. A cricket victory could never be a balm for the mayhem unleashed and lives lost, but it had the potential to boost the morale of a nation that was numb with grief and anger. England set India a mammoth 387 to win the game. In more than seven decades of Test cricket in India, not even 300 had been chased down successfully. That told you the enormity of the task. And Tendulkar himself had been chided right through his career for not being a match-winner. It didn't matter that most of these critics opened their mouths only because they knew anything related to Sachin would help them stay relevant. The narrative had stuck, at least in sections of the media. Following an astonishing Sehwag blitz that set up the game on the penultimate evening, Sachin was unconquered on 103 when India chased down the target with a measure of comfort that took the breath away. Facing the cameras on his way back to the dressing room, Sachin took only a second to dedicate the inning to the 26/11 victims.

For me, Sachin was always bigger than five six-hour days on the field, or a succession of 50-over matches that segued into one another. He was India's contribution to the history of world sport, a man who gave the country recognition on the pitch for

24 long years and continues to do so with anything he does. As his biographer, who spent four years writing *Playing it My Way*, recording more than 100 hours of interviews along the way, his 50th birthday was an occasion to celebrate.

But with a ban in place, how would I pull off something special without ruffling feathers? I was determined not to violate the sanction, and in no position to talk to any of the current centrally contracted cricketers. That was why I reached out to my friends—Kushan Sarkar, Arani Basu, and colleagues Trisha Ghosal and Debasis Sen. We would collectively work on a book titled *Sachin@50*, which would have India's best from different fields talking about what Sachin meant to them. It was decided that Kushan, Arani, Debasis and Trisha would contact those cricketers who had special Sachin stories to recount, while I would speak to the other contributors, from across Olympic sports and the cultural domain. That way, we could make the book a testament to how India viewed Sachin, and how men and women from diverse walks of life had been influenced by him.

No such effort could be complete without the involvement of the family. And in Sachin's case, his family had hardly ever been visible in the public domain. Anjali Tendulkar had only rarely spoken about Sachin, and they remain a very private couple. So it was with much apprehension that I called Anjali and explained to her what I wanted to do. She has always been supportive, and after hearing me out, she said she would revert soon. She added that she had hardly spoken about Sachin or written anything about him. I mentioned that the 50th birthday was a special occasion, and that the book would be greatly enriched by her perspective. Afterwards, I called Ajit, Sachin's elder brother, and made the same request. Ajit and I had spent hours together during the writing of *Playing It My Way*, and share a very good relationship. He immediately agreed, and we decided on a time to record his thoughts the following day. I was pleasantly surprised when Anjali called back to say that she would do a piece, and it would be a very personal take. That was exactly what we needed at the start of the book. I wanted to start with Anjali, and sign off with Ajit. Kushan, Arani and Debasis reached out to a number of Sachin's teammates, and no one, absolutely no one, said no. Each of the cricketers they approached—Rohit Sharma, R. Ashwin, Ajinkya Rahane, Suresh Raina, Harbhajan Singh and Jatin Paranjpe—agreed to contribute to the book.

For my part, I approached Sunil Gavaskar and Sourav Ganguly to ask if they would contribute. While Sachin considered Gavaskar his hero, Sourav and Sachin—once a record-shattering opening partnership—continued to be the closest of friends.

The other person I would have loved to speak to was V.V.S. Laxman. Laxman and I had known each other for years, and I had done some of my best interviews with him. But with Laxman managing the National Cricket Academy (NCA), I decided it wouldn't be fair to put him under the spotlight. While Laxman might have found it difficult to say no, I was hesitant to ask. We decided to settle for a quote instead.

Soon after I messaged Gavaskar, he called me back.

'This is the 500th request that I have received to do something for Sachin's 50th birthday,' he told me in his typical wry humour. 'I have said no to 499. But with you, I will not say no, for I know you will do it well and do justice to the man. Leave it with me, and I will send you my piece.' Within four hours, Sunny bhai had sent me a 1400-word feature, which was a fantastic read. I didn't edit a word of it, and it is now part of *Sachin@50*, published by Simon and Schuster India, which was a bestseller across platforms in India.

Sourav too was just as forthcoming. He first asked what the word count would be and seemed a little apprehensive when I said a thousand. 'That's a lot of words, but let me see what I can do,' he told me. In about seven days, he sent me the copy. The word count was 2,200 words. The article, beautifully written, was a very personal account of the bond the two shared with each other, and was extracted widely by a host of publications.

While each of the contributors enhanced the book, I will refer two of them here—Gulzar Saab and Farhan Akhtar. I wanted to do something special for the back cover, but couldn't figure out what for a couple of months. That was when I decided to call Gulzar Saab, just three days before the book went to press. When I explained to him what I was after, there was a brief pause at the other end before he said, 'Don't you think you could have given me a little more time?' I was embarrassed and about to apologise when he said that he would get back to me within two days. And he did. He wrote a wonderful couplet for Sachin, which we published as the back cover of the book. He was then kind enough to recite it when I visited him at his home in Mumbai, before saying that he had always greatly admired my work. Those words were not only satisfying for the soul, but a reminder that those that mattered remained in my corner. No amount of innuendo or peddled untruths had changed that.

Farhan too was hugely supportive of the book, and we spent close to an hour discussing what Sachin meant to him. He had just recovered from Covid-19, and for him to set aside that kind of time meant a lot.

I informed Sachin of the project just before the book went to press. I wanted him to know that we were doing this, and asked if I could go over and present him the first copy. In fact, I asked Anjali if she would present Sachin the first copy, for that was the best possible way to celebrate his birthday. She agreed, and the plan was hatched. Sachin bought into it, and on April 19, 2023, we visited him in Mumbai to present him the book. He was traveling with the family on his birthday, and this was the best time to meet and spend some time with him. Sachin was extremely warm, and we spent close to two hours at his house discussing cricket and a lot more. He asked me several times about my work, and was very pleased with the book. Each one of the contributors had celebrated him from a very personal standpoint, and that was what made the book so special.

While the visit to his house was extremely satisfying, little did we know that Sachin would talk about the book soon after its formal release. In a tweet, he thanked every contributor for their wishes, and even posted a picture of the two of us holding the book. As ever, the Twitter court tried to derail our efforts. Quite a few questioned Sachin for doing something with me, and some expressed disappointment at how I had managed to find my way back from the wilderness.

At a certain level, it was now starting to become funny. If you read the responses to Sachin's tweet, you could sense the helplessness in a lot of them. How could he do this? Why was he meeting me again? How was it that Sachin had allowed me to compile such a book? Why did quite a few august names from the field of journalism—those like Sunandan Lele, Vikram Sathaye, Neeru Bhatia, Gideon Haigh and G. Rajaraman—choose to contribute to the book? Their peeve, why had I not been buried after I was crucified. The first two reviews on Amazon gave the book a one-star rating, labelling it the worst of its kind. How the readers who posted those reviews could have ploughed through 300 pages in two hours is a question for another day. Since then, the number of reviews on Amazon has grown steadily, and the book now has a 4.3 rating (out of 5) from readers. For close to two months, it was the most-gifted book on e-commerce platforms. Sachin fans and readers alike supported the effort. That I was able to pull it off with so much support from all quarters said a lot, and left me counting my blessings despite everything.

The radio show

On the morning of Sachin's birthday, I had committed to doing a programme for a radio station in Kolkata with one of my favourite radio jockeys, Agni. Agni and I have done a huge number of shows together in the past. However, since the ban, we had not done a single one, and I didn't know whether it was because of the fear of a backlash. So, when Agni called me to ask if I could come over to the studio for an hour to talk about the book, I was pleasantly surprised. When we met, he asked if I was fine with doing a Facebook live on the book. He wanted me to share a few unknown Sachin stories from it with his audience. The moment we started the live, the comments began. For the first five to ten minutes, there were only slurs and abuse. Agni was taken to task for inviting me on to his show. Some of his listeners even said that they would boycott him in future for such a travesty. By sharing his platform with a designated bully, he had committed a heinous crime.

A quarter-hour into the show, however, it began to change. And both of us could sense it. To Agni's credit, he continued, telling me off-camera that he had been prepared for such a response. 'I have never taken the comments section seriously,' he said. 'My job is to do the best show. Let people say whatever they want to.' He also said that he knew the narrative would change after a point, and people's curiosity about Sachin would drown out the cynicism. He was right, and we were live for more than 40 minutes. That night, he sent me a long message saying that the show already had more than 100,000 views, and that the bulk of the messages were positive ones expressing gratitude for the fresh insights about an Indian legend. Since that show, Agni has regularly called me for inputs, something that was routine in the days before the controversy erupted.

On Sachin's birthday, I also got a call from a friend and the Sports Editor at one of India's leading news channels. He was celebrating Sachin on his show with a senior colleague, and asked if I would be willing to go on air with Sarandeep Singh and Dhawal Kulkarni, cricketers who had once played alongside Sachin. After leaving the previous media house where I had worked for almost nine years, this was the first TV show that I had been asked to be part of, and I was initially reluctant because it was going to be in Hindi. My Hindi isn't the best, but I share a degree of comfort with this friend who is the channel's Sports Editor, and eventually agreed to do it. I enjoyed it. Sharing Sachin stories with the audience was fun, and a 24-minute bulletin just flew by. Soon after the show, the friend called back and said, 'Tumne show bana diya [You made the show]. It was an excellent bulletin, and you should do more.' He also said that he had got a few calls asking why I had been invited on to the show. His colleague who had also been on the show had dismissed such callers, saying that I was Sachin's biographer and had also published *Sachin@50*. While things seemed normal and settled on the surface, there were still murmurs backstage. I had been handed a ban and was serving it, yet my life on other fronts was not supposed to return to normal.

This television show was the second occasion when such a thing had happened. Earlier in April, the Abhinav Bindra Foundation invited me to Bhubaneshwar to cover the IOC delegation, which was in India to take stock of the Olympic Value Education Programme (OVEP) that was underway in the state. The delegation, led by Angelita Teo, an IOC director, would be in Bhubaneshwar, and it was an opportunity to document the change that the programme had brought about in the lives of thousands of underprivileged boys and girls in Odisha. I had a long-standing interest in the Olympic movement, and agreed to go. While the visit went very well and the coverage that followed was equally good, I was surprised to learn that a few emails had been sent to the IOC asking them not to work with me. The emails, sent by people I had never heard of, informed the IOC that India's cricket establishment had blacklisted me, and I would therefore be a liability if I was in any way involved with OVEP. The two weren't remotely connected, and it was obvious that the emails were motivated by a desire to hurt my career. Soon after, I called Abhinav to find out if he had heard something similar. His reaction was interesting. 'Have I told you anything about it?' he asked. 'I was the one who had invited you, and I haven't moved an inch from that. Just do your stuff, and let your work speak.'

That was what I did, and the next stop was the WTC final, a match of enormous significance for India, and one that I would be covering from The Oval with the rest of my team. Reporting on an Indian defeat has always been problematic, especially because you are harangued on social media if you are critical of certain players, if even you're backed up by facts. But now, my own personal ordeal, added to the fact that I was a seasoned veteran, and it meant that social media no longer fazed me in the slightest.

I would say what needed to be said and did so from The Oval in London.

10

WTC and Odisha

The World Test Championship final ended at around noon in London on June 11, 2023 and with the result going against India, each of us felt a serious sense of disappointment. I managed to advance my flight and the family and I reached Heathrow by early evening. We had travelled as a family as we did every summer, and as my daughter's school was reopening after the month-long summer vacation, it would help her if we reached Kolkata a little earlier than planned. Sitting in the lounge, I filed my match copy, which largely focussed on India's under-par batting display at The Oval. It was the obvious subject to write about, and I wasn't the only one to do so. The top order had let India down, and it was yet another opportunity lost in an ICC final.

The copy had no mention of The Cricketer, who had not even been part of India's Test squads for over a year. He wasn't remotely relevant to the topic. Yet, soon after the feature went online, the tirades started on Facebook. 'The reason for India's loss was not taking The Cricketer,' said one post in Bengali. 'Show some courage and write that you moron.'

Another went a step further. 'Rahul Dravid has destroyed Indian cricket,' it said. 'Someone who can score 54 in the IPL final could have saved India in the WTC final. The batting collapse wouldn't have happened had The Cricketer played. Write about that if you have the courage to.'

But the pick of the bunch was the third one. 'The Cricketer has helped India win Test matches around the world,' it said. 'Rahul Dravid and Rohit Sharma made the biggest mistake by not including him in the WTC final. And Bengali journalists like (myself) is responsible for this treatment. It is because of journalists like them that Bengal players are continuously ignored.'

There were close to 50 comments in just 30 minutes, each competing to see which could be the most wretched indictment of me. Me, who had no other role in the just-concluded tournament except covering it. It was pointless to try and reason with them. If I had tried to engage as an analyst of the game, and suggested that The Cricketer's prowess was not as a batter, I would only have been trolled further. The Cricketer averaged 27 in 15 overseas Tests, and didn't go past 50 even once in Australia and South Africa. To put that into perspective, the player who replaced him averaged nearly 40 away from home, and had smashed centuries in Australia, South Africa and England. At his age, you didn't expect The Cricketer to get better as a Test batter, and there was nothing in his resume to suggest that he would have mastered a formidable Australian attack in spicy English conditions in early June. And that a 50 in an IPL final mattered even a tad bit. But then, logic is a UFO for online shock jocks, and you would need to be quite daft to take such outbursts with even an iota of seriousness.

With time, the rants gave away to a peculiar kind of victimhood. The Cricketer had made the mistake of picking a fight with me, powerful as I was, and I had consequently conspired to end his Test career. The ban had hardly impacted me, and there I was, traveling the world—proof that The Cricketer, a simple man who knew nothing about politics, had made a mistake.

Whether or not The Cricketer should have been in the squad wasn't relevant to my match report. If you were to ask me now, I would say he could have been after K.L. Rahul got injured. But would he have saved India's blushes? Your guess is as good as mine. But whatever the case, this wasn't something I was remotely concerned with. I was serving my ban, and suffering through it every day. Even for the WTC final I had not applied for accreditation. I had not spoken to a single active Indian cricketer on behalf of RevSportz in over a year and a half, and that had impacted my company. I had, after the ban, initially utilised family funds to pay salaries, and the mental trauma caused by the episode had left deep scars on my family members. To suggest that I had ended The Cricketer's Test career was as absurd as suggesting I could soon become the Prime Minister of India.

There were moments when the itch to answer back was intense. Each person has a patience threshold, and I had reached mine. I was doing my job, and had written what I felt was a very fair match report. India had not batted well, and it was my job as a journalist to lay out those facts.

But then, how could I report on cricket? Rather, how dare I? Wasn't I banned for bullying? Why did the Apex Body allow me to cover the WTC final? How was it that I was watching the game from the stadium, with thousands then watching my broadcasts and reading my copies? I should have been buried and dead, but there I was, at The Oval, doing what I had done for two decades.

Each of these questions was asked. And the language was of the gutters. Was it orchestrated? Was there a puppet-master working behind these faceless cowards? I still don't know. What I do know is that I had mentally planned for each such rant and invective. I knew I would be attacked. And now, I was ready. I had cut short a stint at the Neoma Business School in Paris to come to London for the WTC final. I needed to report on cricket again, and there was nothing in the ban that stopped me from watching cricket in the UK. Or reporting on it from there. I had not applied for media accreditation, and had spent money on buying tickets. A friend who headed marketing for Coca-Cola, had given me hospitality tickets. There were six of us from RevSportz at The Oval, by far the biggest media contingent apart from the host broadcaster. And it was a game plan. While watching the cricket league final, sitting in my brother-in-law's house in London, I had decided that I would cover the WTC final in full steam from The Oval. Each of my colleagues and family members encouraged me to do so. We would be there as a team, and they would all back me up. *Sangbad Pratidin,* one of Bengal's leading newspapers, had partnered with us and that only added to my confidence. While I was a bit apprehensive about getting back to regular on-ground reporting, it was also a challenge that I was looking forward to. Having lived and worked in England for years, I was in a comfort zone, and ready to get back to the buzz of live cricket coverage.

The WTC final and the Asia Cup newsbreak

On day one of the WTC final, I reached The Oval hours before the match was to start. There was the kind of nervous excitement that one feels ahead of a big examination. I wasn't sure if my videos would be watched, or if fans would speak to me as part of the build-up. All those doubts were dispelled within minutes. As soon as we posted the first video, we started getting reasonably good feedback. If there was trolling, I didn't notice it, and there were plenty of Indian supporters at the ground who were more than happy to share their views in front of the camera. Over the years, I had met a lot of regulars at cricket grounds, and some came over and clicked a few pictures. The best was a young boy who was carrying a copy of *Sachin@50,* sent to him by his brother in India. He wanted it autographed by Sachin, and asked me if I could get it done! All of this helped to ease me into work mode. The match was scheduled to start at 10:30 am, and it was around 10:15 am that I made my way to the ICC Hospitality enclosure through the Alec Stewart Gate. The best thing about The Oval was that you could scan your ticket in and out any number of times, and a media accreditation wasn't really necessary in order to work. To my surprise, the Apex Body officials were seated in the row just behind me. There were two of the office bearers, and shortly, another top office bearer joined them. Some members of the Body's administrative team were also there. It was the first time I had come face to face with all of them in over a year.

I should put it on record that each of them was pleasant, and we exchanged polite greetings as soon as we met. With one of them, in fact, I even had a good catch-up chat. It was the first time I had met him since he lost his father, and the conversation turned to issues of mental health. I advised him not to stay alone in the house for too long. No one raised the issue of the ban, and it was as if each of us had moved on. That little negativity lingered among these office-bearers and administrators was evident to me during a longish chat with the Chairman of the Apex Body-appointed committee that had overseen the issue. He was warm as always, and we discussed a host of issues ranging from the cricket league to family. There was no trace of hostility, and the conversation helped us get past the residual awkwardness.

During the tea break, I was to interview Dr Shashi Tharoor, an avid cricket lover and someone I had enjoyed reading for a long time. While I had nothing to do with his politics, Tharoor the cricket fan is a delight to talk to. He knows the game and is especially well read. He was waiting for a cup of tea, and had been invited by an office bearer of the Apex Body for a chat in the hospitality lounge. 'We can speak after I finish with him,' he told me. By then, however, the game would have resumed and neither of us wanted to miss a ball. That was when I requested him to do the interview first, and have his cuppa with the Apex

Body's office-bearer afterwards. 'You tell him that, and then let's go,' he said. I went to the said office-bearer, who was sitting at one of the round tables, and asked if he was okay with Tharoor joining him a few minutes later, after he had finished doing an interview with me. The said individual, a past cricketer and always a polite man, was gracious and said that it was perfectly fine with him. This graciousness was the idea of cricket and cricketers I had grown up with, and what had first drawn me to write on the game.

As we walked down to do the interview outside the ground, Dr Tharoor asked me if things were back to normal. No stranger to controversy, he then made a telling comment, which has stayed with me. I don't know if he remembers it, but he told me something to this effect: 'Just stay true to yourself. Each one of us is answerable to our soul. That's where we are judged. If you know what you stand for, nothing can ever stop you.' I am putting in words here the essence of what he had said to me, for I did not record the exact words. Those words he spoke left a mark. And frankly, that's exactly what I have done. I served my ban in silence while working as hard as I had ever done. Often my silence has been touted as a proof of my guilt. As evidence that I had been put on the backfoot. While time has helped heal wounds, this book is my closure. I decided to go ahead with it knowing full well that it would polarise opinion. I am aware that The Cricketer has always enjoyed public sympathy, and will continue to do so. But this isn't about him. It is my story. It is about sensationalism done on social media, and the harm it caused to someone and their loved ones. And a first-hand lived account of how a social media trial can destroy mental health, lives and careers. And it is proof once and for all from my end that I never intended to apologise and never will. In fact, The Cricketer should, if he feels guilt.

Perhaps I need to digress a little at this point, and speak about a video that I did identifying myself and trying to provide the sequence of events on March 5, 2022. I confess that I did so in desperation. Till then, my name wasn't officially out in the open. I took ownership and came out with the details to provide a perspective to the controversy that was then spiralling out of control. The Cricketer had deposed before the committee earlier that evening, and it was necessary that I too got a hearing. Whether the committee was convinced or not, I needed to point them towards my side of the story. And in the absence of direct access to members of the committee, I decided to put out a video documenting the exact sequence of events. The video was necessary because no one was even willing to hear me out. While it was widely viewed and commented on, the response was overwhelmingly negative. The verdict had already been delivered. It was the only time that I spoke publicly on the controversy. Until this book.

There were 100 or more articles on how my video was not convincing, and how identifying myself was an own goal. I was an easy target, and the more vitriol spewed at me, the better it was for views and TRPs. It was like facing a mob in attack mode. If you read the comments below the video, which are still there, you can see what I am talking about. While a small minority tried to say that I made sense and there was logic behind what I had said, those voices were drowned out. The majority opinion was against me. A few men of standing commented on the video, and asked that I be heard. One was a co-owner of a cricket league franchise. While I remain grateful to him for doing that, he too came under pressure and had to delete his post. We had a long conversation afterwards, and he explained to me that while he was firmly behind me, the post was considered inappropriate because of his status as a franchise team owner. I understood his perspective, and that added to my feeling of helplessness. A powerful man of standing who had invested significantly in the sports domain, couldn't risk siding with me in public. It reinforced just how powerful a force a social media trial could be. The narrative was shaped by so-called influencers, and there was no empathy directed my way.

The video, however, was needed. The dates on my messages had been blurred out before being posted on social media, and small as it may seem, that tinkering set the course that this entire controversy ran. Giving the impression that those messages had been sent to The Cricketer asking for a response AFTER his being dropped from the Test squad, and in those times when any person might not have been in a positive mind space and needn't have been bothered. Those very same screenshots painted him as a victim (of my bullying) taking attention away from the immediately preceding knee-jerk statements on the same social media platform against important office bearers, that might otherwise have attracted the strictest possible sanctions and penalization. The spotlight had been taken off almost-libellous comments against the then cricket establishment. The punishment could have been harsh enough to see his cricket league contract torn up. After all, the league is a tournament conducted by the Apex Body. The bogey of the supposed threat to his career from an aggressive journalist was sensational enough, and raised an emotional pitch in favour of that very same career, and his position in the cricket league, that might otherwise have been severely compromised. Such is the power of social media optics! From being the embittered player who had made indiscreet remarks on social media, he was once again the soft-spoken and honest underdog that fans could relate to. Journalists are storytellers. Only, in this case, I became the subject of the story, for allegedly threatening a cricketer of repute.

I tried to allude to these things in my video. But both life and cricket are about timing. That simply wasn't the right time. I had already conceded ground by staying silent in the immediate aftermath, when I should have lashed out immediately, that very first night, and now there was no comeback. The video was viewed as an attempt at damage control rather than truth. The Cricketer was now an emotive issue—the parameters of the narrative being that the underdog cricketer from relatively modest origins ranged against the globe-trotting (and overbearing) journalist—and it nearly destroyed my family in the process. The narrative was set, and each time he very pointedly insisted that I should have apologised and that I had no remorse (remorse indeed!), we moved further and further into the depths of my vilification.

But the video did serve one purpose. It told people that I would not back down. Despite the beating I took on social media and the damage done to my reputation, I wouldn't back away from speaking my side of the story, no matter what came my way. Perhaps there was a premonition of my rise from the ashes and hence the repeated and periodic observations about my lack of remorse? Maybe to somehow get me to accept the charges and thereby vindicate the accusation? But how could I let that happen? To this day, it gives me great satisfaction that I did not give in at the toughest of moments. With the wellbeing of my family and the company at stake, a compromise that involved an insincere public apology would have been the pragmatic option. Everyone makes mistakes, and I am sure people would have congratulated The Cricketer for teaching me a lesson and putting me in my place, and then leave it at that. Because after all, I had acknowledged my mistake. In fact, several well-established men and women asked me to do just that. 'What's the big deal?' they asked. 'You have everything going for you. Just say you made a mistake and close the matter.'

But where was the justice in that? What about the truth? While the compromise might have helped me materially, it could have had devastating implications for my sense of self. I would always be aware that I had compromised. My messages might have been inappropriately worded in the frustration of the moment, but they were never ever intended as a threat or any kind of harm. By refusing to compromise, I lost the battle. For that moment. But the rage left behind by the injustice meted out to me ensured that I would never lose the war. I have served my ban of 730 days. An unfair one. And now, if even 10 people believe I have a point made, my work is done because I am not here to pander to a mob. In many interviews, The Cricketer had asked why I did not apologise. Through this book, I urge him to come on any public platform of his choice, look me in the eye and face some questions. If he can answer them, I am happy to apologise till the end of time. Let us have a public discussion in front of the media, and put out our respective stories. Let there be a level playing field. He is a good batter. Let me bowl some balls to him for a change and let him hit me out of the park if he can!

While at the WTC final at The Oval, one of the people I met was a dear friend from Dubai. He was an ICC regular and ran one of the major radio networks in the UAE, which also had ICC radio rights for live ball-by-ball commentary. He and I had worked together in 2021, when I commentated on the ICC World T20 for his network in Dubai. My work had caught on with the local listeners, and he had offered me a long-term contract and a substantial sum of money to do the same during the Indian cricket league in 2022. But as with several other contracts, the trail went cold soon after the controversy. Though a friend, he couldn't risk a backlash by having me on air, and a former cricketer was hired in my place.

I met him in Dubai in June 2022, during my book launch. We had an hour-long discussion at his house and he explained his compulsions to me in a most gracious manner. He had to see things from a businessman's standpoint. I was a high-risk resource, and it was best to stay away from me for a while. At The Oval, however, he seemed delighted to see me. We gave each other a warm hug, and spent a fair bit of time catching up. His wife was there as well, and we both recalled the many breakfasts at their house in Dubai. He did mention work. I was no longer persona non grata, and we both agreed that we should combine forces in the future.

The WTC final went extremely well as far as work was concerned. The videos were watched by thousands and the written copies widely read on the RevSportz website. Our website, which had just 421,000 hits in early 2022, had grown to over five million hits in June. Google Analytics had picked up a number of our features, and there was a lot of buzz around RevSportz and the work we were doing. We were covering multiple sports with passion and commitment. And now, we were back in the cricket space as well. The one news item that really helped build that buzz was a story we did on the Asia Cup and the hybrid-hosting model proposed for it. In the media world, breaking news is always a good way to engage, and this was an important snippet. While most news channels, cricket websites and newspapers reported that the hybrid model had been rejected, RevSportz was the only platform to consistently assert that the Asia Cup 2023 would indeed be played on that basis. There was no question of India traveling to Pakistan, and this was the only option available. If the entire tournament had been relocated to Sri Lanka, Pakistan would have walked away from the ACC, which may not have survived such a body blow. The hybrid model allowed India to play all their matches in Sri Lanka while making room to stage a few of the games in Pakistan. It was a face-saver for the PCB, and a way out for the ACC.

During the cricket league final in May 2023, however, there were a huge number of news items that said the Apex Body had rejected the hybrid model. News agencies made it their headline, and it spread like wildfire. I had information to the contrary, leaving me in a bit of a spot. Should we just go with the news flow and put out what everyone else was saying, or did I trust the information that I was privy to? That was where the WTC final helped. As I was walking out of The Oval on June 7, I met one of the ACC's senior most functionaries, someone who had done wonders for cricket's growth in his country. A much-respected administrator, we had known each other for a while and even done some shows together.

Once we got talking, the obvious question concerned the fate of the Asia Cup. 'You are an intelligent man,' he said to me. 'The foremost intention of the ACC is to ensure that the organisation doesn't break down. If that means India takes the position of a lenient big brother, they will do it. India is the nerve centre of world cricket at the moment, and as the leader, they need to take some reasoned calls. While it is not politically feasible for the Indian team to travel to Pakistan, they also need to protect Pakistan's interests and allow some matches to be played there. ——— is an astute administrator and knows what is good for the game. The hybrid model is the only acceptable solution and that's what will happen.'

I had my story. But I still needed a little more detail. I asked him about the likely venues the ACC were zeroing in on. 'Again, let me ask you the same question,' he told me. 'You have been around for a long time, so you tell me. You can't play in the UAE in that heat. Maybe 20-over cricket, but 50 overs a side in September is out of the question. It is unfair on the players, and it isn't something the ACC would do. Oman has similar weather, so that too isn't an option. Nepal—the rains are at their peak, so we can't go there. The same is true of Bangladesh, where it will pour in September. So what does that leave us with?'

Sri Lanka was the only option and the hill country, Kandy to be precise, looked to be the ACC's choice at the time. When I said so, my source gave me a warm smile and said, 'You have your story, but I haven't given it to you.'

On June 7, RevSportz mentioned Kandy as the possible host city for the Asia Cup, while adding that the hybrid model would soon be ratified by the ACC. The story went viral, and a number of my friends in the media asked me if I was sure. *Sangbad Pratidin* carried the story in Bengali, and it was only after we published the story that other websites and news outlets followed. Within a week of us reporting the story, the formal announcement was made, saying that the Asia Cup would be played according to a hybrid model with matches divided between Pakistan and Sri Lanka. The first India-Pakistan game would be in Kandy, with Nepal also playing India at the same venue.

What that WTC final also did was reinforce the belief that we were on the right track. We were being watched and appreciated, our content was being read and shared, and that now applied to cricket as much as it did to Olympic sports. With most mainstream sports eager for in-depth coverage, there was suddenly more work than ever. The ban was no longer an albatross around my neck, a belief firmed up by a trip to Odisha in July 2023.

Odisha—the new cradle of Indian sport

I have now travelled to Odisha nearly a dozen times in the last two years, and each time I have been to Bhubaneshwar, I have been amazed at what is being done for sport. The Kalinga Stadium precinct is now unique. Having taught and covered sport across the world, I can confidently say that there is nothing like it in Australia, the UK or the USA. That's what makes Odisha the new sports hub of India, and things will only get better in the months and years to come.

During one of my trips in mid-2022, I had the opportunity to meet Vineel Krishna, Secretary Sport, Government of Odisha. The visit was coordinated by Hockey India, who were working on a documentary on the history of Indian hockey. As a historian of Indian sport who had documented the history of hockey, I was asked to go and share my perspective.

After the formal interview was over, Mr Krishna asked me if I was free for a few minutes before I returned to my hotel. I had heard a lot about the work he was doing, and welcomed the opportunity to have a chat and understand his vision.

'Please come to my cabin, and let us have a cup of tea,' he said in his baritone voice. Just as we sat down, he added, 'We are aware of what happened, and it is my duty to tell you this. There shouldn't be any apprehension on your part. We know what you stand for, and only after careful consideration have we called you here. We value your contribution to sport, and feel that if you now do a little more work on Olympic sport, it will seriously help other sports in India.'

I was taken aback, for this was the last thing I had expected to hear. The truth is that I was apprehensive, and had expected the topic of the ban to come up at some point. That it did in a manner like this was, however, quite unexpected.

Since then, Vineel and I have become close friends who recently co-authored a book that documents the Odisha sports story, with a foreword by Shri Naveen Patnaik, the Chief Minister of Odisha. RevSportz has worked on a series of documentaries on how Odisha has taken the lead in transforming Indian sport, and at every step, we have received fantastic support from Krishna and the Odisha government.

He was generous enough to invite me to the final of the 2023 Hockey World Cup in Bhubaneshwar as a guest of the government, and I contributed as much as I could to the hockey documentary. There is also a plan to host the 2025 Trailblazers Sports Conclave in Bhubaneshwar, something that we have already started work on.

Over the last couple of years, the Odisha connection has become stronger, and I am delighted to be associated with such a transformative story. In a sense, it was the controversy that made it possible. Had it not been for what happened, I would have continued to do most of my work in the cricket realm, and not really explored Olympic sport in the same manner. While covering the Asian Games or the Olympics, the coverage would never have been as granular as that for, say, a cricket World Cup. Now, it is. RevSportz has covered able-bodied and para sport in equal depth, and documented the exploits of India's leading sportspersons across multiple sports in path-breaking ways. And, more than anything else, it has given us great pride and joy to be able to do so. The impact of what we are now seeing in Odisha will be felt over the next decade, and the book co-authored with Vineel Krishna will always be the starting point for anyone wanting to understand such an uplifting story.

11

Vindication of Faith

During the two years of my ban, the event that I was most apprehensive about was the World Cup on home soil in October 2023. It was the biggest cricket event in India in years, and to not be able to do my work in the manner that I was used to was going to hurt a lot. It wasn't a level playing field with the sanction still in place and I was starting out with a serious handicap. When I compared the Cricket World Cup to the Asian Games, for instance, I knew as a team we would do well in the latter. We have established ourselves as credible players in the domain and athletes know what we stand for. Hundreds of stories and interviews in the last two years bear testimony. However, when it came to cricket, my team was weakened without me being able to lead from the front and make the necessary connections. Cricket in India is a cluttered space and for us to be able to do well, we needed to think out of the box. How could we shape the narrative, for example? Set the tone for the World Cup coverage? Other, more established media houses had more money and resources to deploy on the ground. We were two years old and still relative newcomers to the story. And yet we aspired to compete, so the question was how we did so with the sanction still in place.

We had many meetings on the subject as a team and decided to focus on ground reportage. We would place the fans at the core of our coverage, for sport is ultimately about them. We sent our reporters on every cricket tour, including a relatively low-key one of the West Indies in July 2023, and tried to cover important ground. But then, it was not just about staying afloat. It was about setting the agenda. We wanted our stories to be picked up, discussed, debated and written about. We wanted to lead.

My strength was the connections I had built with some of the legends of the game, men and women who weren't currently contracted cricketers in India, but who continued to define the cricket narrative in India and beyond. These are faces people wanted to see and listen to, and whose opinions mattered. The truth, however, was that none of them came cheap. Each was a star and RevSportz did not have the money to afford any of them yet. Having worked in the domain for decades, I had a clear understanding of the kind of monies we needed to bring them on board, and the reality was that we simply did not have those kind of funds in August-September 2023. So it all boiled down to my personal network. Should I reach out to former players and legends based on relationships formed over the past twenty years? And even if I did, could I even expect them to respond positively, in the context of all that had happened?

One of the first people I called was Gautam Gambhir. Gautam is a good friend and a straight talker. If he did not want to do it, he would say so to my face. And that was fine by me. We have known each other for years and have spoken to each other often in the last 24 months. He was aware of what had actually happened and knew my side of the story. I consider him one of the most astute analysts of the game and someone who has helped India win two World Cups. For a World Cup series, few could be better. Further, I have forever maintained that we don't celebrate Gautam's 97 in the 2011 World Cup final as much as it deserved. While we celebrate M.S. Dhoni's innings and the winning six, and with good reason, it was Gautam's knock that had laid the foundation for MSD to come in and win it for India. What does it take to play an innings like that under pressure when India had lost both Sachin and Sehwag? And that too on home soil? What does it take to score 75 in a World T20 final against Pakistan?

With Gautam, you get answers. He will not sit on the fence or say things in a roundabout manner. Ask him a straight question and he will give you a direct answer. That's what you need on a chat show, and so Gautam was the first person I called.

Gautam was receptive as always. He heard me out in detail and asked when I wanted to record. No money talk, nothing. It was agreed that we would record the show on a Saturday evening when he was relatively free to do a deep dive. I needed Gautam to put things in perspective for my audience. For that, I needed to ask him all the relevant questions. It couldn't be a rush job and was only possible when he had time to think and answer every question. It wasn't a news byte I was asking for. I was asking for a long 30-minute chat where nothing was pre-scripted. He made things easier by saying I could ask him anything I wanted. And that time wasn't an issue. He was doing this to help and wanted the series to go well. Very Gautam. If he believes in something, he will definitely do it. Many feel he is headstrong and has strong opinions. He does, but that's what makes him the man he is. He doesn't give diplomatic answers, and as an interviewer that's what you ask for.

In fact, as the interview started, I had very little talking to do. Gautam was intense and passionate and gave me heartfelt answers. Exactly what you need as a host. When I asked if he felt that his 97 in the 2011 World Cup final wasn't celebrated enough, his response was fascinating: 'I have never thought about it that way. I did not play for stats. They don't matter to me. Had I got a zero and India won, I would be okay. If I got a hundred and India lost, I would never be happy. So the 97 means a lot to me because it helped India win the World Cup after 28 years. Coming to the question, if it has been celebrated enough, not just my 97. Do we celebrate Yuvraj Singh enough for what he did in the 2011 World Cup with all the health concerns he had? Do we celebrate Zaheer Khan's opening spell enough? To start off a World Cup final with four maiden overs is incredible, and yet he isn't given enough credit. Do we celebrate Sachin Tendulkar's efforts enough? Yes, we celebrate him and the win but how many remember he was the highest scorer in the World Cup with two hundreds to his name? While we celebrate M.S. Dhoni's innings in the final, we should celebrate these other efforts as much. No one innings could win India the trophy. It was a collective effort and should be celebrated as such. It is because of social media that we don't do it. Social media is biased and we all know that. But social media doesn't make it the truth. There is always a tendency on social media to celebrate individuals more than the team. In doing so, what happens is we don't celebrate key performers who had as much a part to play. And that's a serious issue.'

As Gautam spoke, I thought about what had happened to me. Social media had decided I was guilty. There was no reason or logic behind this. But once done, it was the established narrative. Just like Zaheer gets pushed behind a little bit, though his efforts in the World Cup final were less than nobody's.

As the interview ended, Gautam asked me if I was satisfied. He knew the interview was important for me and had done it as a show of support. He then said something very significant offline, 'You asked me about pressure. Playing the World Cup final was not pressure. I had runs behind me and I was doing something I liked doing and I was confident of doing well. But when in 2014 I got three consecutive ducks for KKR in Dubai as captain, that's when I felt pressure. I then got 1 in the fourth innings and was ashamed of my efforts. That was pressure. You feel the pressure when things don't go well for you. Not when things are right and you are on a roll. In the fourth match, I asked Manish Pandey to open the innings and batted at no. 3 myself. Manish was scoring and I did this because I was scared. However, Manish was out without scoring and I got out for 1. I told Manish I would never again do this and decided to take things head on. Yes, I was insecure. I was feeling the pressure. I was nervous. But then that's what mental strength and courage is all about. You need to face up to the toughest challenges. In our next game I opened the batting and smashed the first ball from Kane Richardson for four. Perhaps the most important four of my IPL career. That's what it is all about.'

To borrow from Gautam, I had things going my way for the best part of two decades. My books and the corpus of my work between 2002 and 2022 speak for themselves. I had won multiple awards and had done hundreds of interviews with leading sportspersons. I had covered multiple Olympic Games and cricket World Cups and was, in every sense, successful. However, the controversy threw me off gear and damaged my mental health and family life. All of a sudden, I was under pressure. Unpleasant questions were asked of me and my ethics questioned on social media platforms, where ethics and ethical conduct is the rarest animal. My career and livelihood were at stake. My columns were stopped and contracts terminated. Like Gautam, it was my time to step up and show courage of conviction. To give a response to the allegation that I was a bully. In my domain, this book was the best way I could have responded. It is my bat and ball rolled into one. And just like Gautam was mighty pleased with his efforts for KKR, I am very satisfied with what I have been able to do in this book. Offer my truth.

Sourav Ganguly

Sourav Ganguly very rarely opens up in an interview. He is used to giving short answers and you are always left asking for more. When I called him to request time to shoot an episode of *Backstage with Boria* ahead of the World Cup, this is something I mentioned to him. 'Please go into detail. People want to hear from you. The understanding of the game is what I need to get out of you. Unless you open up, the interview will not work,' I remember requesting him. All he said was, 'Come over to my house and we will do it.'

Sourav was no longer a stakeholder in cricket's administration, and hence there was no bar in doing the interview.

It was fixed for a Monday afternoon at his Behala residence and our team reached his house by noon to set up. The refurbished ground floor drawing room was the perfect location and we were all very happy with the frame. Sourav came in around 12:45 pm and looked surprised to see the set up. 'You want to record today,' he asked. I was stunned and said 'Yes,' an emphatic one. 'Arre, today let's just have an adda. You haven't come in ages and now that all of you are here and I am also not working the next few hours, let's all have some food and talk. I will surely do the interview. In fact, let's fix a time today for Friday this week and we can record on Friday,' he said. With Sourav, it is difficult to say no. He seemed in a fine mood and immediately started surfing his phone before telling us, 'How about noon on Friday? This time won't change and you don't need to ask me. Just come by 11:30 am and set up on Friday,' he smiled.

We nodded in agreement. That's when he looked excited and asked, 'Fish fry khabe? (Will you all have fish fry?)...I haven't eaten mishti in ages. It is all very regulated now. And see the results are showing!' Sourav in a good mood is one of the best guys to chat with. We spoke about the intensity of the Ashes and about Anderson and Broad. We spoke about the Indian tour to the West Indies and an interview with Sir Garfield Sobers that our colleague Debasis had done. 'I saw the interview with Sir Gary. You guys are everywhere. Remember what I had told you. There are times when you will get tested. Things may not go your way. But if you stay strong and work with singular focus, there is nothing that can stop you,' he said to me again with a smile.

Our friendship, and I am conscious of using the term 'friend' here, has only grown over the last two years. During his playing days, we shared a mutual respect. Since he has retired, we have become friends. And now it is even deeper. Sourav knew what had happened. He knew that I was subjected to a social media trial. He has tried to be supportive in whatever way it was possible over the last two years. This interview, just ahead of the World Cup, was yet another example.

As we wrapped up the hour-long conversation, pure Bengali adda if my readers know what I mean, I reminded him of his commitment to record, Friday at noon. 'Don't even ask. Just come and we will do it,' he said as we walked out of his Behala mansion.

Sure enough, on Friday morning he messaged. 'We will do it at noon. Please come,' read the WhatsApp message. And it was an excellent interview with Sourav making some very important points about how to approach a World Cup. He spoke at length about Rohit Sharma and Rahul Dravid, about Virat Kohli and the importance of Jasprit Bumrah. He recounted his own leadership career and what he did ahead of the Pakistan match at Centurion in March 2003. He clearly helped set up the

World Cup for RevSportz. The interview was very well received and was widely picked up and dissected across mainstream and social media.

For me, this was the first Sourav interview in 21 months, as the last time that I had spoken to him on record was in December 2021. It was an important conversation for two reasons. It is one thing for a legend of the game to be supportive in private. It is a completely different thing to come on my show and do an interview ahead of the World Cup. He had sent me a video in March 2023 ahead of the RevSportz Sports Conclave, as a wish for the success of the event, and now this interview was evidence of what he felt about me. Sourav spoke to me because he wanted to. The same is true of each and every athlete and cricketer that I have interviewed in the past. And for me, the Sourav interview just ahead of the World Cup was vindication of my work in cricket.

Just as we concluded the interview something funny happened. 'While you and I haven't spoken, I have always spoken to RevSportz,' said Sourav. 'At one level I can't say no to Debasis for he will come up to my room and convince me. And the other thing is you guys are doing fantastic work across all sports. I am sure each and every athlete will want to support you,' he concluded. Those words had a magical effect on my team. We work in a 24-hour news cycle and don't really get to know what stars of stature like Sourav feel about our work. And it is a rare instance when a legend of the game speaks so spontaneously to the team. But over the last two years, several other athletes across other disciplines have said the very same things to me and other team members. And yes, this is despite the ban. Each one has enjoyed speaking to me. And even tweeted about RevSportz and the good work we are doing. Surely not through me having bullied or coerced them! Not one athlete or player has ever felt unsafe or threatened on my account. The work of the last two years is a vindication of what we as a team, and I myself, stand for.

Shoaib Akhtar

Shoaib Akhtar is a maverick. One of the best fast bowlers of all time, he is all headlines in an interview. In fact, speaking to him is much like facing him! He will come at you relentlessly and when on a roll, he will drive the conversation. Ahead of an India-Pakistan game, Shoaib Akhtar is a real big ticket, someone whom people love listening to and whose statements are opinionated. That's what you want in the news business and Shoaib was my go-to man for the World Cup India-Pakistan special. But Shoaib Akhtar, I knew, is always in demand and gets the price he asks, and it's not something I would be able to offer. So the best thing was to tell him upfront and then leave it to him if he wanted to do the show.

I messaged Shoaib the details of the show and explained what I wanted to do. That was my best option for I was sure he would say either a yes or a no and not keep me in limbo. Within 30 minutes, he replied saying he would call. The contact was established and he had not said no. Another hour later, he messaged saying he was still in meetings and that I should wait for him to think and get back. I was becoming hopeful because he wouldn't have made repeated contact had he just wanted to say no. Finally, he called me the next day at 2 pm India time and was all excited. 'How have you been?' he asked me. 'How is the new venture doing for I keep seeing clips on Twitter?' When I said the interview was for RevSportz and would do much for my World Cup programming, he said in a flash, 'Kab karna hai? [When do you want to do it?]' He added, 'Can you send me a Zoom link in the next two minutes and we can do it right away? I don't want to keep this hanging and if I forget I will feel bad about it. I genuinely want to do this for you so it is best we record now. This is the least I can do to help your company.'.

Obviously this was music to my years. Shoaib on RevSportz ahead of the India-Pakistan game would be a blockbuster. With Shoaib on one side and Saurav and Gautam on the other, what more could I ask for? It would mean I could shape the narrative and set the tone for the big-ticket cricket event in India. That's when I asked him about the money. The moment I did, he started laughing. 'Dada, some things are not about money. There is more to life than money. Just send me the link and let's have a chat. How much time will you need? I have an hour for you,' he said.

For a few seconds, I was stunned. He wasn't saying 10-15 minutes. He was saying let's have an hour-long conversation ahead of the World Cup. Ask anyone in the media and they will tell you, it would be an interview that could help set the tone. And Shoaib's statements did indeed set the tone: 'The World T-20 in Australia was all about Virat Kohli. It was as if the cricket gods wanted him to do something superhuman against Pakistan. For otherwise he couldn't have played that shot off

Haris Rauf. That was the most extraordinary innings played by Virat and even as a Pakistani former cricketer all I did was applaud.' Further, 'Pakistan will be the underdog going into the match against India. In front of 130,000 people and all Indian fans, India will start as the favourites. But that's what I will be telling the Pakistani boys. That just enjoy the occasion and run in. Run in and bowl fast. Bowl your heart out. It is India versus Pakistan in a World Cup match on Indian soil. There can never be a bigger occasion than this in their careers and it is a platform to be a superhero. Whoever performs in matches like these gets cult status in their country. Shaheen Shah Afridi with the spell against India in Dubai in the World T-20 in 2021 became a superstar in Pakistan. That's what an India-Pakistan game can do for you.'

As Shoaib was speaking, I had actually switched off. For a good 10 minutes of the interview, I did not know what he was speaking about. My mind was somewhere else. I was actually thinking that I must have done something right for all these players—Sourav, Gautam, Shoaib, Ian Bishop, Curtly Ambrose, Eoin Morgan, Makhaya Ntini, Brad Hogg, Athar Ali Khan, Greg Chappell—to speak to me ahead of the World Cup. It was my best *Backstage with Boria* cricket series in the last two years and it had all come together with the sanction still in place. All these players are legends in their own right. And some of them are the best callers of the game around. Ian Bishop, Gautam Gambhir, Eoin Morgan and Saurav Ganguly can walk into any commentary panel across the cricket world and for them to set up the World Cup for us was a dream. Also, I can safely surmise that each of them knew about the issue. And yet each one of them spoke to me and not one raised the question of the ban. No one felt pressured and no one felt unsafe. No one was doing anything under duress. More importantly, no cricketer of stature is, or should be, so powerless as to have given interviews under duress or pressure to a journalist. It simply does not happen. The Cricketer mentioned other cricketers who had apparently been pressured by me. If that was the case, why did they not come out and give their testimony? Clearly, there were no such other cricketers, and for that statement alone, I could be entitled to claim damages. These legends coming on the RevSportz platform to speak to me were calling it all out—the entire social media spectacle which had nearly cost me my career, and my family and me our peace of mind and our everything. None of these cricketing greats had any compulsion to speak to me. And yet they did. A few of them even promised to come on the show a second time if I requested them to. They had enjoyed speaking to me. My acid test had proved my reputation was still in place. The support of these legends for the platform that I had nurtured, is proof enough.

The show will go on

The morning after I had completed recording all the 13 interviews of the World Cup series, I messaged the CEO and Head of one of our principal sponsors, asking for a time to update him on the progress of our programming. The said sponsor has been the biggest backer for RevSportz and the presenting sponsor for *BWB* since day one. He messaged back saying he was busy in a board meeting and would call me back the next morning. True to his word, he did, and I updated him about the World Cup series. As I was telling him the plan and the names we had, there was silence at the other end. I thought I had lost him. Then he asked, 'You mean to say you have all of these stars for your series?' I said, yes, I did, and he said something I will never forget, 'It has been a privilege associating with this series. And you can rest assured we will be part of *Backstage with Boria* in the future as well. It is something I am very proud of and I can assure you of my fullest support.' As a start-up founder, there could be nothing more rewarding than hearing this. And for having been able to vindicate this trust in me, through my worst times.

As the conversation went on, I informed him that I was writing this book. He took a few seconds to comprehend what I was saying and then said, 'You mean to say you will put out the real story? If that is what you are doing, please go ahead and do it. It takes a lot of courage to do what you are doing and please know I will be there for you. You need closure. Your family will also need closure. The only way you can get that is if you put out your story. I am very pleased that you have decided to do so. It also shows who was speaking the truth. I knew it then and I know it now. That's why we stayed with you and never said a word. Wish you all the best with the book.'

It was vindication. First from the players who came on my show and now from a much-respected corporate leader who had supported RevSportz through thick and thin. We were moving past the impact of the social media lynching and with just a few months left of the sanction, I could finally see the end of the tunnel.

The only other person who has read parts of the manuscript besides my wife Sharmistha and my editors is Abhinav Bindra, the gold medallist Olympian who works tirelessly for the cause of sport. In fact, I had reached out to Abhinav, to ask if he would read it. I needed a solid sounding board to give me feedback with complete objectivity. Abhinav has the intellectual rigour to do so and is someone I have the highest respect for. He agreed and I passed a part on to him knowing that with him I would know exactly how he felt. Was the book a rant at any point, something I was conscious of and had tried to stay clear of? Was it all making sense? Frankly, was it a story that really needed to be told, or was it just me who felt it was relevant to call out celebrity (here a cricketer) entitlement and social media rabble rousing? I had to put my doubts to rest.

Abhinav came back to me the very same evening. He said he loved it and felt it was a much-needed book and that it needed to be written. He had found it powerful and felt pained to know about the ordeal my family had had to undergo. He too said that I needed closure and the truth needed to be put out there, trolls notwithstanding. The way he said it was much like the perfect shot that had got him the Olympic gold in Beijing. Complete courage of conviction. And no half-measures. I did not need to write a politically correct book. I needed to write the truth. And I have. I have lost a lot but regained myself with the help of friends, my team and my family over these last two years. It has made me more of a fighter than I ever was. Fear of another social media backlash, it seems, has left me. Instead, I feel a lot of peace.

12

The Last Word

This has been the hardest book to write. I had started it with that statement, and as I come to the end, there is not even an iota of doubt in my mind about it. The first question, and perhaps the most relevant that I had to answer was: 'Should the book be written?' I was seeking closure, and in truth, I had also become deeply determined to own that narrative which had turned my life upside down. Writing this book became a way for me to channel my angst and, in a way, find solace in my own story and transform it into a means for personal growth. The process of writing was like catharsis, releasing pent-up emotions, and one that brought incredible insight. Self-expression was punctuated with periods of self-doubt, but in the end an unwavering determination allowed me to tell my story.

While enduring the ban for two years, there was not a single day when I did not think about the incident and feel wronged. India played South Africa in a World Cup match in my city on November 5, 2023, and I was not able to go to the Eden Gardens and watch. I had not missed an international game there since 1981. India played England in that Test, and my father, now no longer with us, took special permission from the school authorities to take me to my first cricket game. Little did I know then that I was being initiated into something that would define both my life and career. I was just five then. I also remember that he took me to the Eden Gardens despite the fact that I had a bit of a fever. He did so because I was desperate to watch India play in my home city. I was asked to wear a red hoodie, and Baba stayed by my side because he wasn't sure if I would be okay. But I couldn't miss a cricket match. The seeds of a lifelong obsession were planted very early on.

And now, when my city hosted a World Cup semi-final, I had to do my shows from inside the confines of a studio 20 minutes from Eden Gardens. My colleagues joined me live from outside the stadium. I might as well have been a million miles away.

Bengal played the Ranji Trophy final at the Eden Gardens in December 2022, and again, I couldn't go and watch. The ground which had been almost a second home for 40 years could not open its gates to me.

For the first few months, I was plagued by anxiety. How would I make a comeback, and could RevSportz, my company into which I had sunk my life's savings, survive the negativity? How could I convince people of my truth? And what response did I have to the most damaging statement—that I had actually made somebody feel 'unsafe' through my behaviour?

RevSportz had been created to serve Indian sport, especially in an environment where sport was synonymous with cricket. The aim was to disrupt the status quo and document every Olympic discipline and major sport with the same passion and commitment. But this incident had poured cold water on those ambitions. In front of the committee, I had been alluded to as if I had some kind of criminal background, whereby I could make a person feel 'unsafe' enough to take a different car (and not his own) to the airport. To those that knew me, such a story was laughable, but RevSportz had to function in the public domain, where these allegations had been swallowed whole.

Over time, however, it became apparent that all was not lost. This was a blip, a significant one. But two decades of hard work couldn't be wished away by this surge of negativity. My friends, who had seen me work diligently for years, didn't walk away, and most sponsors continued to back my vision.

New contacts like Vineel Krishna came forward to support the effort. Instead of the ship sinking, RevSportz grew from a seven-member team to a group of 37 that included several very senior and distinguished journalists. Its beauty lies in it being a platform for and by journalists. The number of shows, and the breadth of coverage, has quadrupled. It now has investments that allow us to be on location at every major sporting event—the only Indian platform to do so. RevSportz has showcased every Indian Olympic and Paralympic athlete, and documented their stories. The World Cup cricket series of *Backstage with Boria,* aired between August and October 2023, is still talked about. We may be new to the sports-media space, but there is already a substantial corpus of quality work to fall back on.

What's the point of this book then? Publishing this will give the controversy fresh oxygen, and make it a cause celebre on social media. It will polarise opinions, and give the trolls fresh ammunition. When all is said and done, and I am back in the grid, why step back into murky waters again? I have asked this question of myself every day during the writing process. And had the very same conversation with my wife. And each time, the answer was straightforward. Words are my only defence and armour, and the book had to be written for the truth to be set free. I don't know how many people will believe me, and I do not care too much about the disbelief. But I do know that the truth cannot, or should not be subverted. Friends, acquaintances and even complete strangers, like the gentleman in Singapore, repeatedly asked me why I didn't apologise and move on. It was the easiest thing to do. Perhaps it was imagined that The Cricketer's frequent interviews and social media posts would pressure me into saying sorry. Nobody could have been more wrong. If anything, it made me see the pattern—the pattern of the web that had been spun around me. I was pushed off the stage and prevented from doing my work. I did not need to draw attention to myself by raking up a dead issue. I do so because a narrative is only needed when there has been a miscarriage of justice. Then, it is a risk worth taking.

There will never be an apology. The Cricketer's words, accepted as a verdict by the kangaroo court of social media trolls, led to me being humiliated and insulted for months on end. But no matter how bad things got, I had no intention of apologising for something I never did. I never approached The Cricketer with a compromise. I said as much to the committee. '_____ stated that he has been asked to apologise to the Player, but he will not apologise as he feels he has done nothing wrong,' said their report. 'He sought justice from the Committee.'

I always praised The Cricketer for his skill, and the many interviews we did are proof. I sided with him when he was down and out. Those messages are still there as proof. Remorse? An apology? Not from me.

Instead, it would be interesting if The Cricketer could answer some of the questions I have asked in the book. If he wants to have a conversation in the public eye, where we can ask questions of each other, I'm all for it. I would love to know how exactly I made him feel unsafe. Or why he changed cars to go to the airport. Having known me for over a decade, what was it that prompted these allegations before the committee? If I had been pressuring him for years as he claimed, why had he tolerated such intimidation being a person of eminence and social standing? And why did he then choose to open his mouth on the day he was dropped from the Indian Test team? When the committee heard him, I wasn't there to respond in person. No lawyers from my side were present to rip that narrative to shreds. With the full force of social media behind him, and the trolls baying for my blood for apparently being so entitled, I was crucified. And though the ban is now over, the stain this left on my reputation cannot be washed away. Nor can my distress and my family's suffering be undone. Even today there are stray abusers on my social media raking up the controversy with mentions of The Cricketer. It has caused me irreparable damage.

These pages had to be written because not many face a social media trial and survive to tell the tale. Such experiences crush you, and hollow you out mentally. The stigma is such that you're often afraid to show your face, even in those places where you were once a regular. But despite the trauma inflicted on my family and I, we overcame.

Social media, both a necessity and a curse, can make or break you. RevSportz has grown to where it is today because of the power of the world wide web and sharing platforms. People consume the content daily and their engagement gives it traction. It is empowering when your content is consumed and commented on, and when credible brands come forward to support the endeavour. But the other end of the spectrum isn't as pleasant. The kind of unmediated abuse that has become almost routine on social media is unrivalled. No one can stare down the troll army, because you mostly don't even know who they are. All you see is a comment dripping with malice, sarcasm and then, pure hatred. It isn't too different from the medieval practice of stoning someone to death. In a mob, no one knows or cares who pelts the stones. The trolls come at you in wave after wave. Once you're in the firing line, there is no respite. Even if you were not posting or commenting on cricket, a faceless blob of hatred could still pop up, start calling you names and question your parentage. Having faced that flak for two years, I am now used to it. I had two options in front of me. I could have left social media and insulated myself from the relentless barbs. Many suggested that it would be the best way to stay sane. Nothing would happen if I deleted my X or Meta handles, and stayed off social media for a year. Others suggested that if I did not want to leave social media, I should at least mute the notifications and spare myself exposure to the abuse. But with RevSportz in its nascent stage, neither step seemed feasible. It is a digital-first company. If, as Founder, I couldn't be on social media myself, what would I tell my team? Leaving was not an option. I could either block the trolls on my timeline or hit back. For the time of the ban, I mostly ignored what was said, but all of it registered. This book is the definitive response.

Sharmistha

The most impacted by the entire issue was Sharmistha, my wife. She has always been a very strong-willed lady who has seldom been impacted by the ups and downs in my career. Neither of us was new to controversy, so when things first unfolded, she was the stronger of the two and felt it would soon blow over. Each time we discussed the worst-case scenario, she would tell me that I might be cautioned for my outburst and the chapter closed. We knew that though my WhatsApp messages had been an emotional outburst and not aptly worded. I had done nothing of the kind that was alleged by The Cricketer (threatened him). We were also aware that the widespread outrage on social media could force the Apex Body's hand. But not once did she imagine that I would be banned, and my career put at risk. A two-year ban at that, for sending a WhatsApp message that had been spun out of context. When the ban was announced, she was stunned. Knowing that she needed to stand by me and, most importantly, insulate our daughter from all the negativity, she took control of things at home. Sharmistha had never taken an interest in sport, and our careers were as different as they could be. She is a scholar of Indian cinema with a PhD from the University of Chicago, and an accomplished fiction writer. And yet, in May 2022, I had to tell her that she needed to host the launch of *Maverick Commissioner*, a book on Lalit Modi and the IPL, and moderate a panel discussion on the same. The less time I spent on stage, the better. At the time, we had no choice. She had the intellectual rigour to step up, and did so for my sake. The launch was a spectacular success thanks to her, and it gave me direction. After that, I asked her to accompany me to the Commonwealth Games in Birmingham and join RevSportz formally as partner and COO. She anchored the shows on women's issues and mental health. It was not her comfort zone, but she didn't have a choice. She wanted to see me back in the fray, and this was the only way. We hardly spoke of anything else, and barely even went out socially for these two years. RevSportz became like another child for us and we had to save it at all cost. Everything else took a backseat. And then, we were desperate to put out our story. This book is as much for her as it is about me and a social media trial. No one goes on trial alone. Your family ends up in the dock with you. Often, they suffer more than you do. Research now suggests that when someone is seriously ill, the mental health of the caregivers is as adversely affected, if not more so. It becomes a shared vulnerability.

That's what it was like for Sharmistha. She was used to me being a jovial extrovert. All of a sudden, I was confined to my studio, not speaking to anyone and not doing much. She was the bridge between me and Aisha, our daughter, tasked with trying to paint the picture of a normal household. When I look back, I realise how unfair that was. To see her pictures on social media with crude and vulgar comments was the nadir. To see her get called names for being married to me was gut-wrenching. And yet, she stayed strong through it all. At no point did she break or let me go to pieces, always telling me there was much more to our lives than social media. Or even this ban. And more than anybody else, she wanted this book to be written. Not once did she impose that wish on me, telling me every time to think it through because I would again be in the firing line. But I remember her rush of joy when I overcame my doubts and made that decision. This was her fight as much as it was mine. The same goes for this book.

Aisha

She was just eight then, and did not understand much. And we weren't about to drag our daughter through the muck to try and gain public sympathy. We tried to insulate Aisha as much as we could, but it wasn't always possible. When you are depressed and in no mood to engage with anyone or anything, how do you convince your daughter that everything is alright? Aisha and I had a routine every night that involved reading stories to her. There were days when I would tell her inspirational stories from sport. These invariably brought a smile to her face. There was nothing I loved seeing more at the end of my day. For a year or more, all of this was affected. While she would come and ask me to read to her, I couldn't always bring myself to do so. My mind was somewhere else. I was always distracted, and Aisha did not really know what was troubling me. Even when I forced myself to tell her stories, my thoughts would track back to the issue and what might happen in the future. Now, she knows it all. Whatever little she has understood, she is sure of one thing. Her father would never lie to her. And I know that deep down, she is proud of who she is, her identity, of being her father's daughter. She is proud of what I do and what I stand for. When she grows up and reads this book, she will know the values of steadfastness and courage that mattered to me. That her Boy, as she calls me, did not compromise on those for material gain, regardless of the outcome.

Mamoni (my mother)

My mother, like all mothers, always wanted to see me happy. The well-being and happiness of her son and daughter were of paramount importance. And also her granddaughter. She lost her husband when she was 49, and it wasn't easy for her. She was diagnosed with diabetes at 51, and has been on insulin for nearly 20 years. But the one thing that defines her is discipline. She has kept her diabetes in check, and never let things get out of control. She is 74 now, and still very active. She reads a lot, and has gone through every single fragment that was published against me. At the time, she was visiting my sister in Chicago. Her blood sugar shot up to 273 just a week after the ban. Didi did not tell me then. There were still hundreds of Covid cases around, and she was terrified of what could happen to Mamoni. She knew that I would be a mess if she told me. Mamoni was her usual self only after she got back to Kolkata. She saw us in front of her, and was relieved. Her son was still standing, and trying to work. Her granddaughter was still smiling, and going to school. And by the end of June, her diabetes was back under control.

Each time I think back to that time, I am livid for what happened to my mother, and what could have happened to her under those circumstances. I wonder if The Cricketer, with his declarations about not wanting to harm anybody's family, ever gave thought to my family before each of his interviews wherein I was labelled as remorseless and non-apologetic. Did he imagine that a mother would have to see her son abused every day on social media, or portrayed as a dog with a leash around his neck? Did he ever wonder how she felt, to see her son characterised as akin to a criminal who did his work through coercion? Or my wife or sister for that matter? Did he know, and did he care? If one didn't, I would suggest that defines them as an individual.

Rochona

Rochona, my sister, is a cancer survivor and one of the bravest people I know. When she went through her 16th session of chemotherapy, which left her fingers bleeding, I remember her telling me that she still wanted to write more books and that cancer wouldn't be able to drag her down. She has done so, and I am very proud of her. Now cancer-free, she is the Chair of the Department of South Asian Languages and Civilisations at the University of Chicago. At the time this issue cropped up, she was still undergoing treatment. I can only imagine what she went through. She had to comfort our mother, who was with her in Chicago, and she knew her brother was struggling two continents away, hemmed in by social media walls of abuse. And simultaneously, she had to see off cancer's challenge.

In-laws

For days on end, my in-laws did not go to a single family function. Each time we asked, the answer was the same. 'Your father isn't well,' my mother-in-law would tell Sharmistha. It was only in October, when things started to settle down, that the truth came to light. 'Every family member would ask the same question,' she said. 'What will happen to Sharmistha now that he has been banned? What will they do? We did not want to encounter such questions anymore, so we stopped going.' And yet, at the peak of the crisis, my father-in-law begged me to accept a contribution to my company RevSports at a time I was unsure if the sponsors would remain with me. While I refused the offer, those words of kindness from a father figure are my lifetime's assets. My brother-in-law, a senior investment banker in London, faced similar questions from colleagues and friends who followed cricket. I was the subject of gossip, and my likely fate was a theme for a post-lunch or tea-time chat. It was driven by either pity or a desire to know more. The truth was I needed neither.

Last words

As I said earlier, a social media trial can break you. It forces you to draw on every last bit of inner strength, and yet leaves a permanent scar. I wanted closure in the form of this book. But no one knows better that there will never be closure. I will not get back the two years of opportunities that I lost, or the days and evenings when I was almost a stranger to my daughter. For two years, Sharmistha and I never had a quiet dinner where we could just relax. There was not one evening when we didn't discuss the issue and the book. Which outsider can quantify the impact on the mental health of my family? On my wife? I became cynical about a number of things, and it will be tough to change that. Writing this book drained and exhausted me. The truth is that the incident changed me, my life and my family. There is no going back to what we were. This was our long Covid.

And it was all because of a desperate act of sensationalism on social media. Sensationalism that created a filter for questionable outbursts against two of Indian cricket's legends post the selection for the Indian test side. This act unleashed social media's vermin on my family and me. He is an accomplished cricketer. You don't play over three dozen Test matches for India if you're not. I have had a good career, but will never enjoy the kind of public profile he did by virtue of playing for India. But what has defined me is my resilience in the face of the deepest crisis that I have faced over the last two years of my life. And I can still look my daughter in the eye and tell her that I am speaking the truth.

Acknowledgements

I wouldn't be able to write this book had some people not been there for me at my darkest hour. First and foremost is my wife who suffered unfair abuse and insult for days and weeks and yet held me together. To her, I owe this book and a lot more.

My mother and sister both stood by me every second of the way despite their medical issues and it has only got us closer.

My daughter, who hardly understood the seriousness of things when they unfolded, is happy to see her father smile again. What she doesn't understand is I live for her.

To all my colleagues at Revsportz—Debasis, Trisha, Vinod, Umakanta and our team of 40—you know the truth and stood by it. It takes courage to do so when you are faced with an avalanche of vitriol.

To thank Nalin Mehta would be unfair to our friendship. Nalin has been a brother, and he and Nitika stood by Sharmistha and myself every time we needed that support.

To all my friends and partners—Arnab Roy, Sanjiv Navangul and Vighnesh Shahane—you wrote in my favour when it mattered the most. Forever indebted to you all. Pullela Gopichand and Abhinav Bindra were two people from the sporting world who held me together, explained to me the life lessons from sport and made sure I did not give up.

TV Narendran and Chanakya Chaudhary—their support allowed me to explore newer domains and today we can look back at the oeuvre of work with immense pride.

Vineel Krishna—Odisha and the work being done was salve for me during troubled times. I could immerse myself into work I love doing and forget about the trolls and the abuse.

Vivek and Anil Singh and everyone at Procam—remember asking you in 2022 if you wanted me to continue to host the marathons and all you did was smile and say I am integral to them. Was salve for a troubled me.

Rahul Srivastava and Sayantan Ghosh from Simon & Schuster—you backed me every step and made sure I could muster the courage to tell my story. I am thankful to you both. I must also thank Abhay Singh at Simon & Schuster for his support and positive energy.

Srinjoy Bose, Rajarshi Ganguly and Arinjoy Bose—to the many conversations in your office. Sumeli Chatterjee and Kaustubh Jha—thank you for believing in me.

Kushan Sarkar, Abhishek Tripathi, Arani Basu—to the many phone calls of support and more.

Suddhasatva Banerjee—my deepest gratitude.

I also need to thank Erum Kidwai, Sagar Daryani, Muralikrishnan, Vikas Singh, Karthik Raman, Sarvesh Kumar, Gagan Agarwal, Partha Nandy, Manik Debnath, Gourab Mukherjee, Prantik Mazumdar, Adille Sumariwalla, Imran and Sania Mirza, Neha Rastogi, Nandini Kumar, Chirodeep Bhattacharyya, Rahul Todi, Tamal Ghosal, Shyam Srinivasan, MVS Murthy, Krishnesh Suresh, Kaushik Ghosh, Gautam Bhattacharyya, Abhijit Sarkar, Bhaskar Let, S Prasannarajan, Sudeep Paul, Dipta Mishra, Dinesh Chopra, Anilava Chatterjee, Joydeep Mukherjee, Jaideep and Sharmin Mukherjea, Subhayan Chakrabarty, G Rajaraman, S Kannan, KP Mohan and Vivek Prabhakar Singh for their continuous support and Udita Dutta for being a sounding board.

Indrajit Hazra and Amit Chaudhary—sincere gratitude.

Sanjiv Goenka—for the quiet word of assurance. Joyneel Mukherjee—for dragging me out of the house when all seemed lost.

Ravi Ashwin, PV Sindhu, Rohit Sharma, Harbhajan Singh, Gautam Gambhir, Parthiv Patel—a sincere thank you.

Sachin and Anjali Tendulkar—appreciate everything you both have done for me.

To every troll who abused me—you only made me stronger.

Finally, to Oxford—which allowed me to pick up the pen once more and rediscover myself yet again.